Bigger

BLACK LIVES

———

Yale University Press's Black Lives series seeks to tell the fullest range of stories about notable and overlooked Black figures who profoundly shaped world history. Each book is intended to add a chapter to our larger understanding of the breadth of Black people's experiences as these have unfolded through time. Using a variety of approaches, the books in this series trace the indelible contributions that individuals of African descent have made to their worlds, exploring how their lives embodied and shaped the changing conditions of modernity and challenged definitions of race and practices of racism in their societies.

Bigger

———

A LITERARY LIFE

———

Trudier Harris

———

Black Lives

Yale University Press | New Haven and London

The Black Lives series is supported with a gift
from the Germanacos Foundation.

Published with assistance from Jonathan W. Leone, Yale '86,
and from the Louis Stern Memorial Fund.

Yale University Press books may be purchased in quantity for
educational, business, or promotional use. For information,
please e-mail sales.press@yale.edu (U.S. office) or
sales@yaleup.co.uk (U.K. office).

Set in Freight Text type by Integrated Publishing Solutions.
Printed in the United States of America.

ISBN 978-0-300-26932-1 (hardcover : alk. paper)
Library of Congress Control Number: 2023949181
A catalogue record for this book is available from the British Library.

This paper meets the requirements of ANSI/NISO Z39.48-1992
(Permanence of Paper).

10 9 8 7 6 5 4 3 2 1

FOR ALL OF MY UNIVERSITY OF ALABAMA PhDs:

Delia D. Steverson
Briana Whiteside
Ashley Burge
William P. Murray
Barry M. Cole
Sondra Bickham Washington

CONTINUE TO THRIVE

Depictions of Home in African American Literature
(Lexington Books [Rowman & Littlefield], 2021)

Martin Luther King Jr., Heroism, and African American Literature
(University of Alabama Press, 2014)

The Scary Mason-Dixon Line: African American Writers and the South
(Louisiana State University Press, 2009)

Summer Snow: Reflections from a Black Daughter of the South
(memoir; Beacon Press, 2003)

South of Tradition: Essays on African American Literature
(University of Georgia Press, 2002)

Saints, Sinners, Saviors: Strong Black Women in African American Literature
(Palgrave/St. Martin's, 2001)

The Power of the Porch: The Storyteller's Craft in Zora Neale Hurston, Gloria Naylor, and Randall Kenan
(University of Georgia Press, 1996), Lamar Memorial Lectures

Fiction and Folklore: The Novels of Toni Morrison
(University of Tennessee Press, 1991)

Black Women in the Fiction of James Baldwin
(University of Tennessee Press, 1985)

Exorcising Blackness: Historical and Literary Lynching and Burning Rituals
(Indiana University Press, 1984)

From Mammies to Militants: Domestics in Black American Literature
(*Temple University Press, 1982*)

CONTENTS

———

A Reason to Read . . . ix

A REASON TO READ . . .

———

R EADERS WHO OPEN BOOKS want indications of where the author will take them. In this book, I want you to go on a journey to see how Bigger Thomas, the major character in Richard Wright's *Native Son* (1940), came into being and what his life has been like for the past several decades. In *Bigger: A Literary Life,* I show how Bigger was inspired by Wright's having grown up and lived in Mississippi, by Wright's complicated family life, and by the social, political, and racial circumstances that prevailed in the United States, and especially in urban, ghetto areas in the North, as Wright composed the novel in the 1930s. Mississippi in Wright's youth was a racially restrictive environment that confined Black people to the lowest rungs of society. Wright developed strategies for fighting against that oppression both within and outside the communities in which he lived. He observed Black folks who acquiesced to their conditions and young Black males, the "Biggers" of his environment, who fought against it and suffered the consequences for having done so. Wright thus conceptualized Bigger Thomas against the backdrop of his own life as well as lives he observed around him. He thereby gave "birth" to a character who has engaged readers and scholars for almost a century.

How Black males were treated historically in America was especially relevant to Wright's creation of his character. I revisit briefly the new forms of slavery that influenced the author's portrayal of Bigger, such as the convict lease system, Jim Crow laws, and the sharecropping system. The sense of place for all Black males, but especially for Black males in relation to white women, is relevant for what Wright created as well. A history of lynching with accusations of rape as the primary cause is especially relevant. So is the employment history for Black males in America, especially their consignment to menial jobs and their inability to join unions in instances in which they were fortunate enough to obtain jobs that had union representation. Stunting of personality and life opportunities serves as the historical base for what Wright depicts in *Native Son,* and I want to be sure that readers are aware of that history.

I also show the ways in which a criminal case in Chicago influenced the final creation of Bigger and the role that another writer played in keeping Wright abreast of that case. The richness of that material and Wright's work at the South Side Boys' Club, where Wright encountered northern young Black males who matched the defiant ones he knew in the South, solidified his conception of Bigger. However, the pathway to a novel was not easy, for there were editors, agents, and reviewers in the publishing world who at times questioned Wright's vision of and for Bigger. Wright had to persist through some compromises before he could give his creation to the world, and he had to persist through some negative responses to his creation once the novel appeared. It is fascinating from the perspective of the twenty-first century to see how Wright took on his contemporary reviewers, how he "wrote back" to them on more than one occasion to challenge their readings of *Native Son.* His eagerness to read reviews from the Communists in whose writing club he had honed the skills to produce *Native Son* is also noteworthy.

Since Bigger represented such a dramatic change from previous representations of Black characters in African American literature, I place him in the context of his literary "brothers" and "sisters" who appeared in fictional texts prior to his arrival. I imagine what those characters would think of Bigger and how they might interact with him; in turn, I envision how Bigger might react if he were placed in the fictional circumstances in which they find themselves. I design this speculative exercise to emphasize what a shock to the body of literary creativity Bigger Thomas was when he appeared in 1940. His difference instituted what became known as the Protest Tradition, a form of literary complaint about Black living conditions in America that was designed to inspire predominantly white readers to use their power and influence to bring about change. Such changes would extend to all American citizens the implicit equality inherent in democracy. Wright thus intended Bigger to perform various forms of cultural work.

The path to such performance was not always smooth. I showcase through the decades from the publication of *Native Son* to 2024 how readers and scholars responded to Bigger, how critical trends, politics, and international events all led to varying perceptions of Bigger Thomas. In the 1950s, for example, Americans generally were more concerned about the Korean War than they were about a young Black man in Chicago decrying his status as an outsider to mainstream American culture and opportunities. By contrast, the 1960s and the Black Arts Movement brought renewed interest in and a nationalistic perspective from which to view Bigger Thomas. I argue that Bigger would fit nicely into some of the militant sentiments expressed during the 1960s. He would also be ripe for the kind of mental transformation that proponents of the Black Aesthetic wanted to instill in Black people who had for too long been content to accept the status quo. The literal violence that Bigger commits gets matched in the 1960s with symbolic descriptions of violence as Bigger joins those younger writers and characters in expressions of desire for change in America. I note that some literary characters from the 1960s and later serve well as Bigger's "offspring."

As he marched through the decades on his way to becoming a classic character in American literature, however, Bigger had to undergo various challenges. One of the most stringent came with the institutionalization of feminist interpretive approaches to literary texts. Feminists found much to criticize about Wright and Bigger. Some accused Wright of hating Black women and subjecting them to inexcusable violence; by contrast, they believed, he elevated white women and portrayed Black men as seeing those white women as the ultimate prizes. Thus, even though Bigger claims that he hates the white Mary Dalton, he nonetheless desires her, whereas he uses the Black Bessie Mears merely as a sexual outlet and ultimately bashes her head in with a brick. These critical commentators recognized, however, that, even as they complained about Wright's treatment of women, especially Black women, they were nonetheless assisting in the process of solidifying Wright's reputation in the realm of fictional creation.

A major part of that creation is the narrator through whom Wright gives us Bigger Thomas—at least most of the time. That narrator "talks" a lot. But Bigger has some crucial things to say for himself. I allow him to do so by offering a section in which I focus exclusively on his speeches and comment on them. Those utterances enable readers to see as much of an unfiltered Bigger as it is possible to see given the hundreds of thousands of words that the narrator uses to follow, analyze, and speculate about Bigger. In allowing Bigger to speak for himself, by pushing that narrator slightly offstage, I hope to give readers a chance to think in different ways about a violent and emotionally abusive character. It enables me to ground Bigger in cultural patterns that many critics have accused Wright of not using. What Bigger says for and about himself adds a dimension that urges readers to see a sensitivity, a vulnerability—and perhaps a softness even—in a character whose better traits are at times overwritten by the verbosity of the narrator.

For all the efforts to abort him, for all the drama surrounding his birth, for all the decades of ups and downs of reader and scholarly responses to him, Bigger has persisted. He has persisted through challenges, complaints, and compliments. He is always there, eager for the next generation of readers and scholars to turn their intellectual energy to contemplating his character and actions. He has inspired countless articles, books, and bibliographies, special issues of journals, a plethora of theses and dissertations, and numerous regional, national, and international conferences. He has inspired fora for public policy. He has inspired movies and television shows. Indeed, for all his faults, for all his violence, for all his antisocial behavior, Bigger has arguably become an ambassador, for he is a source of cooperation across countries and cultures, whether that is American scholars teaching Wright and *Native Son* in China or European scholars attending conferences on Wright in the United States. Bigger has led to comparisons to the conditions of young Black men on American soil in the twenty-first century, evoking Michael Brown, George Floyd, and a host of others. Bigger Thomas is, then, a character for the ages, a fictional creation whose birth has led to longevity but who remains the twenty-year-old whom Wright gave to the world more than eighty years ago. What has happened to him since is quite a journey, one that I highlight in the pages of this book.

I invite you to take this journey with me.

Bigger

INTRODUCTION

———

A FEW YEARS AGO, a colleague at another university re-counted an incident surrounding her teaching of Richard Wright's *Native Son* (1940). When the discussion reached the point in the story where Bigger Thomas, a Black man, kills Mary Dalton, a white woman, and burns her body in the furnace, the professor asked students if they could identify and possibly understand the extenuating circumstances that resulted in Bigger's actions. How might growing up in a ghetto with severely limited life opportunities, which meant that Bigger was excluded from the promises of American democracy, have affected his behavior? How might systemic and historical treatment of Black males have informed his actions, especially in those intense moments in which he reacts instinctively to the circumstances in which he finds himself?

The answers students provided, together with the professor's own comments, led one white female student to report to her parents that her African American professor was suggesting that it was "all right" for Black males to kill white females. The back-lash was immediate. My colleague said the incident gave her such pause that she almost gave up teaching. How, she pondered, could such a serious misunderstanding have occurred? How could the student have so blatantly misinterpreted the intent of the discussion? That anecdote has stuck with me all these years because it captures vividly the visceral as well as the intellectual response to Bigger. Can a young Black man, living on the South Side of Chicago, ever earn sympathy after such an egregious act? Even if readers reject him, can the sequence of events that led to Mary's death be understood? For all the social and political issues Wright raises in the novel, that super-violent cross-racial interaction between Bigger and Mary remains at its center, and Bigger remains in the American literary imagination as a monster or a victim, or some combination of both.[1]

The situation with Mary is horrific enough; however, Bigger then compounds that atrocity by raping and killing his girlfriend Bessie Mears when she becomes reluctant to follow through with the flimsy kidnapping plan he devises to account for the white girl's disappearance. Bessie has been most sympathetic to Bigger and is the person to whom he has gone for physical and emotional comfort before and after Mary's death. Murdering Bessie thus takes him several notches up the scale of monstrosity to which many readers and scholars have assigned him. Even though Mary's death might have been accidental, no such explanation applies to Bessie's demise. Bigger's bludgeoning of Bessie is pure, cold-blooded murder, which he convinces himself is necessary to prevent her from revealing his whereabouts to the police. What happens to Bessie, therefore, can never be separated from Bigger's legacy of violence, never excused, and never viewed in the light of any extenuating circumstances that may have been applicable to Mary's demise. Thus Bigger, Mary, and Bessie form a bloody triangle that has saturated the intellectual pursuits of critics and scholars since Wright gave them to the world in 1940.

In 2020, *Native Son* turned eighty years old. What, over those eighty years, was the journey like that enabled Bigger, despite his complex and despicable actions, to find a home and become centered in American and African American literary studies? What history and politics shaped Bigger's creation, either in the social arena or in Wright's own life? What did Bigger's creation reveal about the state of African American literary creativity in the first third of the twentieth century and prior to that? Who were Bigger's ancestors and relatives? How was Bigger welcomed into the world on March 1, 1940? What were the immediate reader and scholarly responses to him? Into what camps of criticism or politics did those responses fall? How have readers, scholars, and critics responded to Bigger over the past eight decades? Were there points at which this viciously violent young Black man was more accepted than at others? Why? Were there points at which he was rejected—or at least criticized severely? What accounts for those reactions? What impact has Bigger's characterization had upon Black writers who followed Wright, especially Ralph Ellison and James Baldwin? If there are other literary Biggers, what has been their scholarly or political fate? This volume seeks to answer these questions and others by articulating what a literary life of Bigger Thomas contains.

* * *

At 576 typescript pages, *Native Son* was the longest novel any Black writer had produced. Wright divided his lengthy creation into three parts: "Fear," "Flight," and "Fate." In "Fear," readers meet the Thomas family, which consists of Bigger, his mother, his sister Vera, and his younger brother Buddy. The Thomas family resides in a "kitchenette" apartment building, which means they are confined to a single room with cooking possibilities but with no bathroom in what their landlord has lavishly called an "apartment," mirroring the lives of many Black migrants from the Deep South during the Great Migration of the first half of the twentieth century.[2] Wright makes clear from the beginning that the Thomases are victims of economic, political, and social circumstances that slot people of African descent into lesser positions in American society. In the novel's famous opening scene, Bigger corners a huge rat in the apartment, kills it with a skillet, and dangles it in front of his sister until she faints, thus marking the fate that will become his own as the novel progresses.

A combination of willingness to protect as well as willingness to harm, Bigger appears shiftless and drifting, preferring to hang out with his gang. Social services has made it clear that the only way they will continue to support the Thomas family is for Bigger to get a job. Though the family pressures him to accept the job he has been offered as chauffeur to the rich, white Dalton family, Bigger deflects them and, instead, leaves the apartment to hang out with his friends at a local pool hall, playing at petty theft, and going to the movies. In his interactions with his friends, Bigger experiments with moving from the "boy-ness" that America uses to define Black males to some state of manhood, as he attempts that path through verbal aggression and violence.

For lack of anything better to do, Bigger decides that he will indeed go to the Daltons and interview for the job. His movement from familiar territory in the Black neighborhoods of the South Side of Chicago to the superrich space of the Dalton home allows readers to see the contrast between an at times confident Bigger and a Bigger who is thoroughly uncomfortable—both with the expansive space in the Dalton home as well as with the pleasant manner in which he is treated. This pleasantness that leads to discomfort is compounded when Mary Dalton enters while her father is interviewing Bigger. She is overly familiar and disregards all the cues about white female interactions with Black males that have governed Bigger's life.

Bigger's discomfort worsens on his first night in the job, when he chauffeurs Mary and her Communist boyfriend, Jan, who act in ways that violate all protocol that governs Black chauffeur/ white rider interactions—and, what's more, Jan drives Mary and Bigger to a Black restaurant, where Bigger sees his erstwhile girl-friend Bessie. Afterwards, Bigger drives around the park while Mary and Jan drink and make out in the backseat. This ahistorical situation leads to expressions of hatred that Bigger feels toward both of these young white people for making him so uncomfort-able. Their intentions might be good, but they are ignoring every-thing that has governed Bigger's life before he meets them.

Later, after dropping Jan off at a subway stop, Bigger drives Mary home, only to discover that she is too drunk to find her way to her bedroom. This begins the fateful sequence of events that spurs the novel forward. Bigger helps Mary to her bedroom, hears the blind Mrs. Dalton approaching, and puts the pillow over Mary's face so that she will not speak and give away his presence. When Mrs. Dalton departs and he removes the pillow, he discovers to his horror that Mary is dead. Shocked, frightened, and desperate, he takes her body to the furnace room, decapitates it, and puts it in the furnace. He arrives at a state of calm, takes Mary's money-stuffed purse, and returns home. He is asleep within "five min-utes" of getting into bed.

Notably, words such as "fear," "feared," "fearful," "scared," and "afraid" saturate the first section of the novel. That fear is often as much generated from within as it is from without. Bigger the potentially violent young man and Bigger the fearful, scared young man parade through the first section of the novel.

The second section, "Flight," documents the sequence of events leading up to Bigger's attempted escape. It begins with a Bigger who seems to have no regrets about his actions of the night before. His secret gives him a newfound sense of freedom and perhaps even superiority, as well as feelings of benevolence toward his friends and family. He returns to the Dalton home and acts out the part of carrying Mary's trunk to the train station for the trip she was scheduled to make to Detroit and waits to see how the Daltons will respond the longer Mary is absent. In addition, Bigger attempts to implicate Jan in Mary's disappearance; since Jan is a Communist, Bigger assumes that the Daltons and their private investigator are only too willing to believe the worst about him.

This section of the novel chronicles Bigger as he visits his girlfriend Bessie, who becomes his unwitting, and then his coerced, accomplice in a scheme to present Mary's absence as a kidnapping and to pose as the kidnappers and collect the ransom money. Bessie's part in the plot is the third point of the violent triangle that the novel draws. A work-worn domestic for whom alcohol and sex with Bigger are the only things that sustain her monotonous life, Bessie is skeptical about the scheme but feels forced into it, then distraught, then increasingly afraid.

Bigger delivers the ransom note to the front door of the Dalton home, where Peggy, an Irish immigrant who is housekeeper, cook, and loyal servant to the Daltons, discovers it. Bigger watches as Mr. Dalton reveals the note saying that Mary has been kidnapped and as reporters hungry for information will not leave the Dalton basement. Soon, blazing newspaper headlines report the kidnapping. Here is one of the novel's turning points: reminding himself that he could escape at any time, Bigger realizes that, for the first time in his life, he has choices. He can go, or he can stay. He can play the dumb darky with Mr. Dalton, Britten (a private detective Mr. Dalton has hired), and the reporters, or he can bristle at their stereotypical assumptions about him and blow his cover of having done something that none of them would suspect a poor Black man capable of doing. He continues to perform ignorance. Then, fate intervenes. A reporter shovels the ashes in the furnace to allow better circulation of heat and finds tiny pieces of human bone along with one of Mary's earrings. At that point, Bigger sneaks up to his room in the Daltons' house, retrieves a gun he has brought there, leaps from a window into the snow, and begins the trek that will result in his capture.

Bigger arrives at Bessie's apartment, maintaining that Bessie will be considered as guilty as he is because she has spent some of the money from Mary's purse, and forces Bessie to flee with him to an abandoned tenement building. A crying, weak-willed Bessie stumbles along with Bigger into the freezing cold building. Her ineptness at becoming a fugitive leads Bigger to conclude that he cannot take Bessie with him and he cannot leave her behind. After they have spread covers on the floor for the night, Bigger rapes Bessie and, once she falls asleep, takes a brick he has spied earlier and bashes her head in. He then drops her body down an airshaft before moving to another spot from the one where he has murdered Bessie. Readers will learn later that this brutality did not end Bessie's life; she froze to death trying to climb out of the airshaft. More immediately dramatic for the plot is that Bigger shoved Bessie down the airshaft without retrieving the money from her pocket. He had given her the remainder of the money from Mary's purse as an enticement to acquiesce in his plot. Now, without funds in a snowy, freezing Chicago, Bigger is on the run without any possibility of leaving the city.

As he treks through the South Side of Chicago, Bigger showcases another level of heightened awareness about the status of Blacks in comparison to whites. His developing political and social consciousness, however, cannot stay the inevitable. Quickly, law enforcement officers and other citizens arm themselves to hunt for Bigger. More than eight thousand white men terrorize Blacks on the South Side of Chicago as they ransack apartments in pursuit of him. Finally spotted on a rooftop, Bigger climbs a water tank in a last attempt to get away from the mob. He discovers that his hands are too cold to even fire his gun. He is at the mercy of his pursuers when a water hose is brought in and he is laced with icy wetness until he slides from the top of the water tank to his capture.

His "Fate," therefore, echoes that of countless numbers of Black males in America who run afoul of the law. There may be brief interludes of eluding capture, but there is no escape, especially not when the crime is against white womanhood. The third section of the novel follows Bigger as he is captured, moved from jail to jail, and constantly confronted with shouts from white citizens demanding that he be lynched. To protect himself from constant emotional assault, Bigger hides behind a shell of indifference. Because he sees no way out of his predicament, he rejects the minister whom his mother sends to comfort him. If the cross represents Christianity as well as the Ku Klux Klan that screams for Bigger's life, then he wants no part of the crutch on which his mother leans.

The preacher is the first of several visitors, each of whom stages a possible alliance or route to salvation for Bigger in his cell. An understanding Jan arrives and offers legal representation through the Communist Party. Jan brings Max, an attorney, with him, and Max takes Bigger's case. The text stretches credibility at this point as the preacher, Jan, Max, the Daltons, Bigger's family, Bigger's gang members, and the state's prosecutor, Buckley, are all present in the cell at the same time. Bigger's actions result in consequences for Bigger's family: the police harass them constantly, and they have been slated for eviction. Although Mr. Dalton joins his wife in stating that he can do nothing for Bigger, he asserts that he will stay that eviction. All the others leave except Buckley, who rather easily gets a confession from Bigger, so easy in fact that he says Bigger is "Just a scared colored boy from Mississippi."[3]

Bigger spends time brooding in his cell or being transported to various hearings. At the inquest that will determine whether or not a trial will occur, he hears spectators outside the building calling for his death. He listens as Mr. Dalton takes the stand at the inquest and understands that the man is naive enough to believe that if the Thomas family lives in a tenement that he owns and pays rent to a third party that he is somehow not responsible for their plight. He also believes that Blacks prefer to live in such neighborhoods with other Blacks instead of in better communities. And he contends that his shipping ping-pong tables to the South Side Boys' Club as an act of charitable liberalism overshadows his real estate practices. The scene moves Bigger from listening to watching, however, when Bessie's nude and brutalized body is brought into the courtroom and displayed as evidence against Bigger. He intuits correctly that the body is used to show the monstrosity of his perceived actions against Mary, and that Bessie ultimately does not count. Returning to the jail, he sees a cross the Ku Klux Klan is burning, which leads him even more vehemently to reject Christianity and its primary symbol of the cross.

After an extended conversation with Max, during which Bigger tries to explain his life and actions, he is finally brought to trial. The trial consists of two speeches—Max's attempt to get a sentence of life in prison for Bigger instead of the electric chair, and the prosecutor Buckley's effort to ensure that Bigger will die as quickly as possible. Max's defense, evoking history, racism, politics, sociology, and Communist philosophy, takes up twenty-three pages of the novel. Readers do not get a sense of Bigger's response until the end, when Bigger registers pride that someone has valued him enough to put forth that much effort for him, even as he knows that the effort will not save him. Buckley's indictment, on the other hand, is a crisp nine pages that mirror the racist, kill-him-as-soon-as-possible sentiment of the spectators in the courtroom and those surrounding the courthouse. Running for re-election, Buckley shouts loudly for a criminal element to be destroyed without the least bit of consideration of extenuating circumstances. As his speech dehumanizes Bigger in the animalistic ways that the mob of spectators has urged and attacks Max as wrongheaded and anti-American, readers quickly realize that Buckley and the majority both inside and outside the courtroom are in agreement; Bigger and Max are outsiders.

Wright thus uses the trial to make a basic point about Black male existence in America. Bigger was tried, convicted, and sentenced to death (literal or figurative) from the moment he was born. Unquestionably, he smothered Mary Dalton to death. However, from Buckley's point of view, Bigger's very existence has made Bigger guilty. As a Black male, Bigger cannot find a place to live in America in the late 1930s and claim innocence. He is always already guilty. His motives are always suspect, and the society will try as much as possible to circumscribe his actions. The trial, then, is a performance designed to accomplish transformation in Wright's reading audience, for the audience in the book has already decided on Bigger's death in the electric chair. It is therefore a surprise to no one that Bigger is sentenced to die by electrocution.

The novel ends with a conversation between Max and Bigger, during which Bigger asserts that what he killed for must have been good for him to feel it deeply enough to kill for it. Max is appalled and cannot stomach such a possibility. He walks away from the cell and barely responds when Bigger asks him to tell Jan that he said hello.

* * *

The clanging of steel against steel as the jail door shuts on Max's departure is the beginning of literary inquiry about Bigger as well as historical inquiry about Richard Wright. Who was this man who conceptualized such a vision? Wright, like Bigger Thomas, was born in Mississippi, on a plantation outside Natchez. His childhood, adolescence, and teenage years were riddled with deprivation, lack of affirmation, and racial repression. It was only after he migrated to Chicago in 1927 that he began to receive consistent support for his creative efforts, but the hunger and deprivation frequently still prevailed on that northern landscape.

The deprivation that Wright experienced in Mississippi was family-related and had multiple layers, though it was certainly informed by the larger economic conditions of the society. Wright's father, a poor sharecropper from whom Wright later became permanently estranged, moved the family, consisting of Wright, his mother Ella, and his younger brother Alan, to Memphis in an effort to improve their economic condition. That move proved emotionally scarring when Wright's father abandoned the family for another woman, which left Mrs. Wright with the responsibility of caring for two young boys in an environment that did not provide the extended family support that relatives in Mississippi had. For the young Wright, hunger settled into his stomach and mind and became the guiding metaphor for his life (his second autobiography, for example, is titled *American Hunger*). His mother left the six-year-old boy home with his younger brother Alan while she worked, which led to Wright getting into fights with white boys (for which his mother beat him severely), as well as to his becoming an alcoholic when patrons in a local saloon thought it was cute to ply a child with drinks. The situation devolved even more when Ella was forced to put the two brothers in an orphanage for a time because she could not afford to support them. Wright was appalled when the director of the orphanage proposed to adopt him.

Wright escaped that situation when his mother took the family to live in Elaine, Arkansas, with her sister Maggie. On the way, they paused in Jackson to visit Wright's grandmother, a devout Seventh-Day Adventist with little tolerance for childhood disobedience or deviance. When Granny caught the schoolteacher boarding with her reading tales of Bluebeard to Wright, she labeled it the devil's work, and the teacher was forced to move. Going to Arkansas provided a brief respite, but it came to an abrupt end when Aunt Maggie's husband, Uncle Hoskins, was shot and killed by whites who coveted his successful saloon business. Wright was nine years old at the time. Aunt Maggie could not claim her husband's body or have a funeral. The women simply sneaked out of town to West Helena, Arkansas, until things quieted down. After Maggie left Arkansas, Ella had a stroke that resulted in Granny's arrival and the return of the family to Jackson, where, in consultation with Ella's siblings, the two brothers were split up and sent to live with their aunts and uncles. In Greenwood, Mississippi, at his uncle's house, Wright was unable to sleep because his first cousin had died in the bedroom now assigned to him. He therefore returned to Granny's house in Jackson.

That arrangement, in which Wright found himself until he left Mississippi as a teenager, proved to be a distinction without a difference, for Wright was just as hungry, physically and emotionally, in this environment as he had been in Memphis and Arkansas. For religious reasons, Granny did not allow her family to partake of certain foods, such as pork, veal, or fish, so there were many times when Wright was forced to subsist on flour laced with lard. Depriving her family of certain foods was mirrored in the grandmother's refusal to support Wright's creative urges. Granny believed that creating stories, as the adolescent Wright did, was tantamount to performing the work of the devil. Stories are "lies," because they are made up, and anything that is made up is antithetical to scriptural directives about telling the truth. Dependent on his grandmother because of his mother's increasing ill health, Wright grew up in a household where he was an outsider. Not only did he alienate his grandmother, but he alienated his aunt, who was one of his teachers at the local school, when he referred to her in class as "Aunt Addie." Addie joined her mother in believing that Wright was spawned by the devil. This was the case with one of Wright's uncles as well, after the boy threatened him with razors when the uncle tried to chastise him.

The family had no place for an independent, gifted youngster who was not as righteous as his relatives perceived themselves. In almost every encounter Wright recorded of his interactions with relatives, he was considered the different one, the one who needed to be contained, the one who would not adhere to the rules by which families should operate, especially in terms of taking the word of elders as law. When he composed his first story and had it published in a local newspaper, no one was excited about the achievement. Even the female classmate he read the story to was puzzled as to why he would write it.

An outsider in his family, Wright was also an outsider in terms of the racial situation in the South. Restricted by geography, economics, and skin color, Wright did not have the proper temperament to survive for long in the South. On one occasion, he interviewed for an after-school job, and when the prospective employer asked if he steals, Wright laughed. That is not the expected response in such a situation. A simple "No, Ma'am" might have sufficed. Laughter, however, evokes suspicion, which illustrates again how Wright was an outsider to and alienated from just about everything and everyone around him. His alienation continued when his middle school principal presented him with the commencement speech he was expected to make as the class valedictorian. When Wright refused and said he would write his own speech, everyone, from the principal to his grandmother to his mother to his Aunt Addie and his uncles, believed that he was simultaneously arrogant and stupid. Such incidents added fuel to Wright's determination to leave the South.

Wright accomplished that feat by taking a job at a movie theater after graduation, then becoming part of a scheme to resell tickets, and saving money for his departure. He also joined a couple of middle-class young Black men who believed it would be good fun to steal goods from a warehouse and sell them. These extralegal activities enabled Wright to fulfill his hunger to leave the South, which he did by making a midway stop in Memphis in 1925. He saved money to continue the journey to Chicago by eating as sparingly as he could, such as running hot water over a can of pork and beans to eat for dinner. This deprivation became critical later, after he arrived in Chicago in 1927, when he had a hard time getting a job at the post office because he was underweight. In Memphis, working in an eyeglass factory, he experienced the intensity of ugly racism when two white men harassed him after he inquired about learning the trade instead of just doing the equivalent of janitorial work. He and another young Black male were also victimized when white men connived to get them to fight each other by telling tales to each about the other. The only good that came out of Memphis was that a kindly white man allowed Wright to use his library card to check books out of the local white library. This privilege enabled him to discover H. L. Mencken's *A Book of Prefaces* (1917); Mencken and his work became inspirational for Wright. Mencken, he concluded, was fighting with words, which is what Wright himself was determined to do.

Although he continued to be economically deprived for years, Wright nonetheless always helped his mother, brother, and aunts. He was not living well in Memphis, but he brought his family from Jackson to join him. A family conference determined that he and his Aunt Maggie would leave Memphis for Chicago, and his mother and brother would follow later. Thus joining the Great Migration, Wright arrived in Chicago to the cold blasts of winter and the kitchenette dwellings that defined the living conditions for most migrants from the South. He persevered, however, by earning as much money as he could, reading and writing into the wee hours of every night, and staying focused on the larger goal of becoming a writer. He persisted even when his aunt felt he was driving up their electricity bill too much by staying up so late reading and writing. He persisted when he moved his mother and brother to Chicago. He persisted when he moved his family from one dingy apartment to another and when he had only a space about the size of a closet that he could call his own. As the primary breadwinner in the family, Wright settled into a role that continued to be his for decades; indeed, once he became a successful writer, he purchased a home for his family in Chicago. Whenever his mother or his aunt needed money, well into the 1950s, they would be in touch with him to fill their requests. It is no small feat that Wright was able to work, house his family, and write.[4]

The writing became easier when Wright connected with the John Reed Club in Chicago and started attending meetings with creative young people. This was his introduction to the possibilities of affiliation with the Communist Party. Wright fed his mental thirst by reading avidly about Communism as he searched eagerly for patterns around the world that would improve the condition of Black people in the United States. He was looking for Biggers, no matter their skin color. He became an intellectual guide to his good friend and fellow writer Margaret Walker, who, like Wright, was an aspiring poet and novelist. Walker credits Wright with introducing her to such works as John Reed's *Ten Days That Shook the World*, Maxim Gorky's *The Lower Depths* and *The Mother*, Karl Marx's *Das Kapital*, John Strachey's *The Coming Struggle for Power*, Adam Smith's *Wealth of Nations*, and *The Complete Philosophy of Nietzsche*.[5] Wright read anything and everything, from history and politics to sociology, biography, novels, poetry, essays, and whatever else would improve his understanding of and ability to interpret the capitalistic, racist system under which he lived. His self-teaching was incredible by any standard of measurement, all of which he achieved with an eighth-grade education. It is no wonder, then, that he was at times shocked and offended when he was portrayed in negative terms as an intellectual.

Wright nonetheless found refuge in the John Reed Club and made a wholehearted commitment to the club and its work. The young white people there seemed to accept him, his talents, and his ambition. Not only did he become a regular at meetings, but he became a leader in the group. He held the position of secretary, and he wrote regularly from the point of view of workers of the world. His in-depth reading about revolutions around the globe led him to believe that the Communist Party offered the best options for Black progress in America. His unqualified embracing of the John Reed Club is perhaps in part a testament to Wright's never having really belonged anywhere before. The John Reed Club provided a kind of home for Wright, and he gave it the best of his mental and physical self. He was crucial to its creative and political work. His poetry and essays were published widely in such outlets as *Left Front, New Masses,* and *Anvil,* and his became a household name. When he joined the Communist Party in 1932, therefore, it was the formalization of a relationship that had existed for a long time. Unfortunately, the marriage did not last.

After a while, some party members became suspicious of Wright because he was too independent; he wanted to write and publish creative materials instead of the propagandistic pamphlets his superiors preferred. One milestone leading toward separation occurred when the John Reed Club in Chicago was disbanded because of internal friction and clamoring for influence and power. Wright was directed to do work in New York. It was there that he discovered more fissures in what appeared to be the solid structure of Communism. In a famous incident, he was not allowed to march in a parade with his fellow workers. On another occasion, he was denied living quarters in a hotel that catered only to whites.

Still, Wright remained in the party as he published *Uncle Tom's Children* (1938), his first collection of short stories. Most of the stories portray Black characters in southern settings who are shut out of the opportunities of American democracy. The collection received praise from most readers, although Wright later perceived it as having been limited politically.

When Wright moved to New York, Benjamin Davis, perhaps the most important Black Communist at the time, befriended him. Davis was an Ivy League graduate, a former athlete, and an attorney. He shielded Wright from criticism he received from others in the party for being an independent intellectual, and he generally encouraged his publications. This relationship later became stressed, however, when Davis offered a mixed, and late, reaction to *Native Son* in 1940. For Davis, as for many other Black reviewers, Wright had made Bigger Thomas representative of the masses of Black people, and that did not set well with them. They wanted to assure the reading public that, although there might have been some angry, dissatisfied Bigger Thomases on the American landscape, they did not represent all Black people. The majority of Blacks, Davis asserted, were willing to work their way into the American democratic promise in more constructive ways. They were not as angry and certainly not as violent as Bigger. As soon as Bigger stepped into the world, therefore, controversy surrounded him, and that controversy continues in 2024.

The bombshell that is *Native Son* was unlike anything the American literary world had seen. Here was a Black male character who violated the most sacred of taboos and then almost celebrated his violation. Bigger performed acquiescence instead of truly believing it. Unlike his predecessors in the best-foot-forward literary tradition that defined most African American literature, especially during the Harlem Renaissance of the 1920s, Bigger is defiant and angry, and ultimately unapologetic. Nothing will appease him short of full-fledged participation in everything that America has to offer. He shatters notions of the "nice Negro" and made the larger society wonder what might be lurking in communities near them. He gave public policy officials fuel for their projects, and law enforcement officials reasons to be more vigilant. Conversations surrounding the best way to assist with Black progress in America joined with those about monsters who could never be contained. The society needed to determine what to do with Black males, for if Bigger Thomas represented even a fraction of them, then the implications for social unrest were expansive.

Politics implicit in *Native Son* and in Bigger's actions underscore the cultural work Wright designed his novel to achieve. No sensitive readers should come away from the text with the same attitude toward race relations that they might have had before reading the book. The novel also solidified its place in African American literary history by making Wright the go-to author for all things Black in America. *Native Son* became the marker of African American literary achievement, when scholars and observers could remark about events "before *Native Son*" or "after *Native Son*." This watershed moment in African American creative achievement stood for more than a decade, and after that the novel would compete well with Ralph Ellison's *Invisible Man* (1952). It was *Native Son*, however, that made it impossible for scholars to view African American literature in the same way. Assumptions about what publishers would and would not print were shattered, for here was a novel that indicted white America vigorously, and it still reached the light of day. Here was a novel with a dangerous, often unlikable protagonist, and still it was published. What the novel portended for publishing by African Americans or about African Americans, therefore, was as important as its subject matter. It was no longer a question of what white publishers would not print, as

Zora Neale Hurston had observed, but how eagerly they could print realistic portraits of African American life.[6]

Wright and *Native Son* instituted what became known as the Protest Tradition, a focus in African American literature on conditions of Black lives that needed redress by the larger society. It led to such works as Ann Petry's *The Street* (1946), and James Baldwin's *Go Tell It on the Mountain* (1953). Both novels are unblemished representations of Black lives, and both reiterate the urban ugliness that defines *Native Son*. With his pivotal work, therefore, Wright shaped arguments for decades about how best to portray African American lives. Baldwin may have shared literary kinship with Wright, but he was also critical of what Wright had done, while Ellison vehemently opposed being slotted into kinship with Wright. Such discussions nonetheless illustrate the impact of *Native Son* and reiterate the poet and professor Sterling A. Brown's comment about the novel when he asserted in an early review: "*Native Son* is a literary phenomenon. Magazines have run articles about it after the first reviews. It is discussed by literary critics, scholars, social workers, journalists, writers to the editor, preachers, students, and the man in the street."[7]

Brown noted further that the nationwide focus on the novel extended to "juke joints" as well as literary gatherings. The literate and the presumed illiterate, Northerners and Southerners, Easterners and Westerners, liberals and racists, all discussed the book. It had such an impact in Mississippi that Wright dared not risk setting foot on the soil there; his friend and biographer Margaret Walker observed, "Wright's relatives in Mississippi reputedly told him not to come home or he would be lynched." The power to capture imaginations, to evoke praise, and to raise the public ire that Bigger exhibited immediately following his birth has continued for almost a century.[8]

A biography of a character is a risky undertaking, for it is always difficult to separate the character from his creator. In Bigger's case, Wright uses a narrator who spends extensive amounts of time translating for readers Bigger's innermost thoughts and feelings. The challenge for a researcher is to get past that narrator and arrive at the essence of Bigger, or at least to minimize the power of that narrator, to cut through the translation of the character into the character himself. Because the narrator is so prominent, it is necessary to parse out what that narrator has to say, take the most relevant kernels, and perhaps put less relevant material into a secondary—though still important—position that reflects more Wright than Bigger. The tasks are heavy ones, because Wright had a very specific agenda with Bigger. He wanted his readership to see and own what American society, in its refusal to live up to its democratic promise, had done to Black Americans, and especially to young Black males. Society had shunted young Black males into a dead-end space—for Bigger, the South Side of Chicago—and thereby limited their life choices significantly, because viable resources for survival and self-actualization in that space were almost non-existent. In order to ensure that his message comes through sharply and vividly, Wright allowed his narrator to take up whatever slack in delivery might be compromised by the twenty-year-old Bigger, who has only an eighth-grade education; and this meant that Bigger feels and intuits more than he can articulate about his own psychology and the forces that have shaped him into who and what he is. Bigger voices his frustrations, and he certainly understands racial oppression, but the deep structures of psychology that are available to the narrator are unavailable to him. When he actually speaks, therefore, readers are obliged to pay close attention.

It is especially important to see Bigger in context, in relation to his family and friends, interacting in daily conversations. Foregrounding those moments in the novel enables readers to see Bigger's aspirations and longings, expressions of deprivation, and cries of exclusion that come straight from the heart. As much as possible, therefore, a life of Bigger Thomas needs to let Bigger speak for himself, even when he may be lying or misrepresenting events. Indeed, even his lying and distortions are significant in understanding what kind of character he is and providing glimpses into a personality that ultimately resists being consumed into the narrator's elaborations. The task of separating Bigger's voice from that of his creator borders on the formidable. Still, even as I seek such separation, I recognize that Wright and Bigger are so intricately intertwined that they can never be separated fully. Nor should they be. Thus, with that caveat, I wade into the mass of contradictions that is Bigger and the mass of creativity that is Wright. Somewhere in the interstices that connect both, perhaps I can indeed arrive at a literary life of Bigger Thomas.

CHAPTER 1

The Birth of Bigger Thomas

WHEN RICHARD WRIGHT published *Native Son* in 1940 and gave Bigger Thomas to the world, he already had a solid, award-winning reputation as a poet, short story writer, and essayist. One of his most memorable poems, "Between the World and Me," about a speaker who witnesses a lynching and then imagines himself being lynched, had been published in the *Partisan Review*.[1] In a nationwide competition, he had won a $500 prize from *Story* magazine in December 1937 for *Uncle Tom's Children* (1938), his collection of five novellas. Early in 1939, he received the O. Henry Memorial Award of $200 for "Fire and Cloud," one of the novellas in *Uncle Tom's Children*, and in April 1939 he received a $2,500 Guggenheim Fellowship to support his writing for a year. His poetry and essays had appeared in a variety of Communist-leaning outlets, including *New Challenge*, which he co-edited when he left Chicago for New York. One essay in particular, "Blueprint for Negro Writing," was commissioned by Wright's Communist superiors; it became an early statement on the aesthetics of Black writing, and is still cited.[2]

Wright often attended Communist conventions and was

frequently asked to deliver speeches that furthered the work of the Communist Party. In 1935, he was offered the opportunity to travel to Switzerland as a delegate to a youth conference, and then to the Soviet Union for study. Wright declined. He saw this as a way for the party to thrust him into a leadership role, when he wanted to be a writer. The incident nonetheless measured the potential the party saw in him. From the vantage point of 2024, it would be reasonable to suggest that Wright in the 1930s was a public intellectual, a much sought after thinker and speaker.[3] His conflicts with members of the party—usually centered on his desire to write in ways they did not prioritize—did not diminish the party's appreciation for his speaking skills or their desire to have Wright represent Communist interests. Also, the party did not want to be perceived as racist by denying Wright opportunities that his skills clearly warranted. To advance his writing agenda, Wright lived a double life in which he worked fervently for the party and equally fervently for himself.

During the 1930s, he completed two novels and submitted them for publication; neither was accepted. The first, *Tarbaby's Dawn*, set in Jackson, Mississippi, follows a character named Tarbaby who runs away to Memphis, and is based on Wright's experiences with an unsympathetic family. The work remains unpublished. The second novel, *Lawd Today* (originally titled *Cesspool*), about life among four postal workers in Chicago, did see publication in 1963, after Wright's death in 1960.

As a young writer eager for recognition, Wright was contemporary with Margaret Walker, who later became well known for winning the Yale Younger Poets Award in 1942 with her book *For My People*. Her novel *Jubilee* (1966) and her poetry are also well regarded. Another contemporary, Zora Neale Hurston, like Wright and Walker, was also trying to earn a reputation as a writer. Although Walker and Wright shared much, Hurston and Wright were at odds about how best to represent Black lives. Hurston sided with working-class, folkloristic traditions that were not designed to elicit the kind of protest that Wright believed crucial to writing, while Wright believed that any intelligent Black writer should use his or her skills for the advancement of Black lives in America instead of merely appreciating them in their current states, as Hurston seemed to be doing. Debates about protest guided writerly and scholarly conversations as a prominent question remained highlighted: should Black writers create as artists first or as Black people first? Wright foregrounded the social and political positions of Blacks, while Hurston celebrated the unique and intrinsic qualities of Black life that were manifest in folk traditions and that did not need white audiences for validation or correction.

By the time *Native Son* appeared in 1940, Hurston had published *Jonah's Gourd Vine* (1934) and what would become her signature creation, *Their Eyes Were Watching God* (1937). She also published, in 1935, *Mules and Men,* folk materials that she had collected in sawmill camps in Florida and among voodoo practitioners in New Orleans. The literary landscape surrounding Wright, therefore, was not one in which vocal protest was the norm. It is easy to see how *Native Son* inaugurated such a tradition. Other writers of the period, like Waters Turpin in Maryland, were, like Hurston, champions of folk lives and folk traditions more than complainers about those lives and traditions. Their protagonists were much more likely to join their comrades in playing guitars and singing in local juke joints than decrying the conditions that birthed the juke joints into existence. Wright therefore was creating against the grain of a tradition even as he might have included characters who could have shared many social circumstances with characters in those works by his fellow authors. Such possible kinship, however, was minimized in the face of Bigger Thomas and his dissatisfaction with the state of American society that excluded

Black people from almost everything. His is a legacy that has lasted far longer than many of his contemporary creations.

Bigger's fatal encounter with Mary Dalton has captivated readers and scholars for nearly a century, despite the shocking, transgressive, and discomfort-evoking reactions the novel elicits.[4] How, then, did Bigger get born? The circumstances of his birth are a fascinating mix of biography, racism, history, custom, and sociology. Wright drew upon his own life as an oppressed Black person in the South to shape Bigger, as well as upon a history of Black male literary representation. He wanted to ensure that Bigger's literary life would be dramatically different from Bigger's Black male literary cousins and relatives. Wright created a character for whom racially inflected considerations shape responses that readers and scholars have had—and continue to have—toward him. In the process of bringing Bigger to life, however, Wright had to deal with a number of publishing considerations and limitations that influenced how his character was presented to the world. He was forced to make compromises that scholars have questioned for decades.

Wright's creation of Bigger was informed by many factors, including reader responses to earlier work by Wright, what he himself had to say about creating Bigger, and the kinds of characters that peopled the African American literary landscape before Bigger's appearance. After Wright published *Uncle Tom's Children*, he found the reviews disappointing. He had created characters who experienced racial, cultural, and social limitations as well as violence in their bids to live freely in a southern society intent upon containing them. Hopeful that these portrayals would encourage transformation in the society these characters were drawn from, Wright learned that, yes, indeed, readers did sympathize with his characters. However, instead of charging up the hill of social equality and demanding that people of African descent in the South and America generally be included, democratically, in what the society had to offer, readers did not move beyond their emotional responses. To them, feeling sorry for the characters proved sufficient, and it did not prompt them into meaningful social action—instead, they could congratulate themselves on "feeling right."

Consider Big Boy, in "Big Boy Leaves Home." One of a group of four boys swimming in the nude in a waterhole to which they have been forbidden access, Big Boy and his friends stare in horror as a white woman, the fiancée of the son of the white man on whose property they have trespassed, comes upon them as they are basking in the sun after their swim. Seeing the woman and frantic to get away, they move to retrieve their clothes, which they have left precisely near the tree where the woman is standing; shocked into immobility, she screams as they approach. Her armed fiancé, arriving quickly and erroneously thinking he understands what he sees, shoots and kills two of the boys. Big Boy then wrestles the gun from the man and kills him before he and his remaining companion, Bobo, escape the scene. History, custom, racism, and a lack of the possibility for transformative communication all coalesce in tragedy. Even though Big Boy and Bobo flee the waterhole, there is absolutely no opportunity for true escape on southern soil. Bobo is caught and lynched, burned to death. Big Boy, after hiding in a hole on a hillside overnight, gets a ride with a Black trucker on his way to Chicago.

Human decency devoid of racism would suggest that the youths deserve sympathetic responses from white readers and that those readers would draw several conclusions, perhaps along these lines: racism is bad; Black people are human and suffer just as non-Black people do; violence is inexcusable; the murder of innocence is horrific and condemnable; communication between Blacks and whites needs to improve; this is an overall sad set of circumstances;

conditions need to change; what can I do to bring about change? "Big Boy Leaves Home" and the other stories were thus designed, in the Protest Tradition that Wright popularized, to elicit social action from readers—especially white readers.

That was not the case. Readers certainly sympathized with characters in *Uncle Tom's Children,* but, as far as Wright could tell, sympathy was a dead-end proposition; it did not migrate toward or spur social action. Of those initial reader responses, Wright wrote: "When the reviews of that book began to appear, I realized that I had made an awfully naïve mistake. I found that I had written a book which even bankers' daughters could read and weep over and feel good about. I swore to myself that if I ever wrote another book, no one would weep over it; that it would be so hard and deep that they would have to face it without the consolation of tears." The first impetus to creating Bigger was thus to ensure that the character had such a hard-hitting impact on readers that they could not stop at the level of superficial emotionalism. Some social action would be the minimum response. The second and perhaps most important spur to Bigger's creation is the character's growth out of Wright's lived experiences. While a couple of years might have served as the immediate gestation period for Bigger's creation, Bigger's genesis was based in the very southern soil on which Wright grew up and the conditions under which Black people there lived. Upon reflection following the publication of *Native Son,* in his essay "How 'Bigger' Was Born," Wright chronicled the inspiration for Bigger's creation.[5]

That essay is simultaneously explanation, reflection, and perhaps too much of an attempt to place Bigger into the arena of world politics. Wright avows, believably, that Bigger was decades in the making. "The birth of Bigger Thomas," he asserts, "goes back to my childhood." After exploring select events from that childhood, he explains how world events, such as the Russian Revolution and

Hitler's rise to power in Germany, led him to realize that there are Bigger Thomases all over the world, both Black and white. "While living in America," he wrote, "I heard from far away Russia the bitter accents of tragic calculation of how much human life and suffering it would cost a man to live as a man in a world that denied him the right to live with dignity. Actions and feelings of men ten thousand miles from home helped me to understand the moods and impulses of those walking the streets of Chicago and Dixie." That political explanation for Bigger undoubtedly has some validity in shaping Wright's thoughts about political conditions closer to home and their impact on Bigger; however, it is also necessary to remember that one character, even one limned as expansively as Wright does with Bigger, cannot ultimately carry the weight of international politics or connect all races and peoples. Clearly, this portion of the essay was influenced by Wright's growing exploration of Communist philosophy and the conditions of workers throughout the world. The essay touches more immediately on plausibility when Wright recounts the numbers of Black males he encountered in the South who had the rebellious attitudes that coalesce in his creation of Bigger.[6]

To show readers that Bigger is not an isolated character cut from the whole cloth of his imagination, Wright identifies five specific Black males who represent types that defied the laws and customs of racial interactions in the South. He states that if he had known only one Bigger, then perhaps *Native Son* would not have come to fruition. Instead, there were many of these rebellious types. The first Bigger was a bully who terrorized younger Black boys in Wright's neighborhood, of whom Wright was one. We need but think of Bigger's alienation from his family, his violent reaction to Gus about the possibility of robbing Blum's, and his general separation from codes of morality to see the connection here.

The second and third Biggers directed their actions toward

defying whites directly, one charging food and clothing and never paying for them, as well as not paying rent to white landlords, and the other barging his way into theaters and not paying. Although Bigger Thomas is reluctant to confront whites directly, the spirit of defiance that informs his responses to many events in the novel showcases his kinship with these historical Biggers.

The fourth Bigger had a "rebellious spirit" that "made him violate all the taboos, and consequently he always oscillated between moods of intense elation and depression." This fourth type anticipates Bigger Thomas by asserting: "The white folks won't let us do nothing." The fifth Bigger, pre–Rosa Parks, rode streetcars and sat in the "WHITES" section; not only does he refuse to get up when the conductor accosts him, but he pulls a knife and dares the conductor to "make" him move. Think of Bigger's pulling a gun on Jan when Jan seeks an explanation as to why Bigger has implicated him in Mary's disappearance; it shows that he has the potential to strike out when he feels cornered, which echoes the rat scene at the beginning of the text when Wright makes clear that Bigger's fate is as sealed as that of the rat.[7]

For their defiance, all of the historical Biggers end up tragically, as Wright concludes: "The Bigger Thomases were the only Negroes I know of who consistently violated the Jim Crow laws of the South and got away with it, at least for a sweet brief spell. Eventually, the whites who restricted their lives made them pay a terrible price. They were shot, hanged, maimed, lynched, and generally hounded until they were either dead or their spirits broken." Wright's fictional Bigger evokes these historical figures in his highs and lows, his moments of elation and depression, the times when he believes he is in control (writing the ransom note) and the times when he realizes that all is lost (when the mob of white policemen pursuing him corners him on a rooftop in the snow).[8]

Not only does "How 'Bigger' Was Born" offer explanations for the creation of the character in terms of history, politics, sociology, culture, and economics, among other things; it also makes note of the gaps in and remedies for creations in African American literature. One need but think of Toni Morrison's comment on her own impulse to write to appreciate Wright's point. Morrison said she wrote the kinds of books that she wanted to read, because, clearly, they did not exist before she created them. Similar testimony has come from other writers, such as Ernest J. Gaines. After scouring shelves to try to find literary representations of African American peoples and cultures, Gaines concluded that he had to produce what was missing. Wright, then, is an early example of this conclusion, for he states that learning from white writers enabled him to do something that he had not witnessed with writers of African descent: "This association with white writers was the life preserver of my hope to depict Negro life in fiction, for my race possessed no fictional works dealing with such problems ['the locked-in life of the Black Belt areas'], had no background in such sharp and critical testing of experience, no novels that went with a deep and fearless will down to the dark roots of life."[9]

Wright thus determined to create Bigger as a kind of laboratory experiment developed from the multitudes of readings and experiences that had shaped his own life and about which he had learned. He comments: "So, with this much knowledge of myself and the world gained and known, why should I not try to work out on paper the problem of what will happen to Bigger? Why should I not, like a scientist in a laboratory, use my imagination and invent test-tube situations, place Bigger in them, and, following the guidance of my own hopes and fears, what I had learned and remembered, work out in fictional form an emotional statement and resolution of this problem?" Wright's experiment is the arduous task of portraying a young Black man who is in American society, but who is shut out from its benefits and rewards, who feels intensely his separation from those around him (both Black and white), who intuits more than he can articulate, who acts faster at times than he can think, and who is always aware of the limitations his society places upon him simply because he is Black. Truly, Wright has created a laboratory and a set of experiments. What would happen if Bigger were placed in situations in which he violated taboo, either accidentally or willfully? How would he respond to those violations and recognition of what they meant in terms of the larger, white society's perceptions of him? Would he be able to manipulate his narrative, or would he find himself victimized yet again by those who would not only write his story but who would kill him in the telling *and* kill him physically? Wright undertakes his experiment and willfully explores that "deep sense of exclusion" that shapes and defines Bigger and everything he experiences.[10]

That knowledge of himself and the world to which Wright alludes and explores in "How 'Bigger' Was Born" is also bolstered in Wright's classic essay "The Ethics of Living Jim Crow." It provides additional illumination into the racial and social positioning of Black males, especially in the South, that went into the conception of Bigger and illustrates yet again how Wright's life influenced the gestation period for *Native Son*. "The Ethics of Living Jim Crow" offers a series of vignettes in which Wright finds himself at the racial mercy and power of whites. From interacting with whites in employment situations, to being the butt of their jokes in hitching a ride, to witnessing a Black woman being beaten for not paying a bill, Wright showcases the ways in which white supremacists in the South shape young Black males to adopt roles and resort to actions that whites then view as deviant and criminal. On one occasion, Wright is working at a hotel and witnesses the sexual harassment of a Black woman. He may be inclined to assist the woman whose hip the white night-watchman casually slaps as she walks past, but realistically there is nothing that he can do. Consider as well the incident in which, working as a hotel "hall-boy," Wright takes a bottle of alcohol to a room where a nude white prostitute is entertaining a "john." He is expected, metaphorically, to blind himself rather than "see" the languishing nude white woman get up from the bed and "waddle" across the room to get money to pay for the liquor. Even the thought of his having actually looked at the woman raises the ire of the john.

> "Nigger, what in hell you looking at?" the white man asked me, raising himself upon his elbows.
>
> "Nothing," I answered, looking miles deep into the blank wall of the room.
>
> "Keep your eyes where they belong, if you want to be healthy!" he said.
>
> "Yes, sir."[11]

In this instance, as well as in other vignettes that Wright captures in "The Ethics of Living Jim Crow," *place* and *space*, both psychological and physical, are integral to Black/white relations in the South, as they will be for the southern migrant Bigger when he encounters a white woman on northern soil. Wright cannot protect the Black woman from the white night-watchman as American society suggests that men should be able to protect the women in their lives. The space of the hotel and the place of the South make it impossible for Wright—*if* he wants to live—to do anything but heartily acquiesce to the insult and indignity that the woman is forced to endure. So, when the white man notes that Wright seems to object to his action, he uses his power to push Wright into submission by asking him if he likes what the white man has done to the Black woman; Wright almost chokes on his inability to offer any other than a seemingly acquiescent response. He recalls:

> One night, just as I was about to go home, I met one of the Negro maids. She lived in my direction, and we fell in to walk part of the way home together. As we passed the white night-watchman, he slapped the maid on her buttock. I turned around, amazed. The watchman looked at me with a long, hard, fixed-under stare. Suddenly he pulled his gun and asked:
>
> "Nigger, don't yuh like it?"
>
> I hesitated.
>
> "I asked yuh don't yuh like it?" he asked again, stepping forward.
>
> "Yes, sir," I mumbled.
>
> "Talk like it, then!"
>
> "Oh, yes, sir!" I said with as much heartiness as I could muster.
>
> Outside, I walked ahead of the girl, ashamed to face her. She caught up with me and said:
>
> "Don't be a fool! Yuh couldn't help it!"[12]

If Wright dares to move outside the psychological space to which whites have assigned him, he risks the consequences of bodily harm.

In the hotel with the white prostitute, Wright has been granted permission to be "out of place" physically by the fact that the white hotel management has assigned him the task of delivering liquor to the woman and her john. That out-of-place physical permission, however, does not extend to any out-of-place psychological permission. Wright must still contain himself, shutter his eyes, and pretend that he does not see what he cannot help but see, for the woman makes no effort to shield herself from him. Comparable to the Battle Royal scene in Ralph Ellison's *Invisible Man* (1952), a novel that has blindness as a central theme, young Black boys who witness a nude white woman being manhandled by drunken white men must pretend that there is nothing unusual about the situation. Seeing but not seeing is just as expected of them as it is expected of Wright. The boys in Ellison's novel are out of place by permission—since they have been invited to entertain the white men by boxing in front of them—but they must retain their psychological blinders even when what they are not to see is strikingly, insistently, in their line of vision.

Being out of place is endemic to Bigger. However, readers need but contemplate three scenes to see how thoroughly this historical concept impacts Bigger. He has been forceful, argumentative, and combative in his interaction with his family just as the novel opens; however, once he leaves the Black space of the South Side and enters the home of the white Dalton family, he is shy, reticent, and strives to make himself invisible. He has not been in a space comparable to the Dalton home, and he can only rely on stereotypical clues about interaction between whites and Blacks to get a sense of how he should act. He is not accustomed to whites addressing him politely; nor is he accustomed to sitting in their spaces and having a conversation with them. And he is definitely not accustomed to a young white woman, namely Mary, being excessively friendly and familiar with him. Under these circumstances, there is no rock of confidence that can provide a place of solidity for his assaulted personality.

The second instance of these spatial dynamics occurs later, after Bigger's interview and hiring by Mr. Dalton, only to find himself woefully unprepared for his interactions with Mary and Jan as he drives them from the Dalton home to the Loop and then rides with them to Ernie's Kitchen Shack. Bigger has no history of pleasant interactions with whites and thus again no basis from which to derive any pattern of behavior that might save him from embarrassment or something more dramatic. He is adrift both physically and psychologically. Being expected to violate the spatial custom of where to sit when riding with whites or being expected to violate taboo by eating with them at Ernie's are but two of the ways in which Bigger is made to feel acutely the consequences of place and space. Significantly, Mary's and Jan's inability to see Bigger, his history, or their combined histories of spatial limitations further foreshadows the later events of that fateful evening. Bigger is figuratively assaulted by liberalism, and he has no defense against that assault. Wright thereby imbues Bigger with the discomforts that he himself experienced and recorded in "The Ethics of Living Jim Crow."

Of course, third, the most striking and reader-engaging violation of space and place is Bigger's entry into the Dalton mansion with the drunken Mary, followed by his entering her bedroom. This is a circumstance, as I argue elsewhere about Big Boy and his friends in "Big Boy Leaves Home," that no Black man can enter, claim innocent intentions, and expect those intentions to be viewed as credible.[13] Bigger finds himself in multiple layers of spatial and psychological violations. Initially, custom dictates his exclusion from this part of the white house. Black people who worked for whites historically had specific spaces designated as "Black" spaces *within* the white household. For Black domestic workers, that Black space was the kitchen. For Bigger, the Black space in the Dalton home is the kitchen as well as the sleeping room the Daltons have assigned to him. His being in Mary's bedroom is the ultimate violation of space, for not only is he a Black male in a white female's most private space, but a history of psychosexual, Black male/white female relationships accompanies him into that space. That history is present in his body, his mind, his every thought, action, and reaction. Bigger and Wright are thus kindred spirits in body and mind as "The Ethics of Living Jim Crow" documents.[14]

By chronicling his own experiences and the racial history that informed them, Wright clarifies the plan for what he hoped Bigger would accomplish in the literary world as well as among readers in the general public. When he figuratively gave birth to Bigger, he could not have fathomed the impact that his character would have upon literary studies almost a century later. The literary world Bigger was born into, however, was one in which the character's rebelliousness is set against a backdrop of mostly gentile characters who are not overtly concerned about upsetting the status quo. In his restlessness, his physical and emotional violence, and his deviousness, Bigger echoes a few African American literary characters, but he is mainly a sharp contrast to his literary brothers and sisters.

Bigger's creation was a stunning break with the African American literary tradition up to this point and signifies one of Wright's great innovations in *Native Son*—a feat on which Wright thought deeply. Despite the fact that Bigger is in a gang, he is not group or community oriented, as was the case with a couple of his predecessors. His anger shines, just as his resentment shines. He basks in his antisocial, outlaw status, as he feels no remorse about the criminal, immoral acts he commits, such as robbing and stealing. He is content to let his racial anger boil and complain about it rather than take steps to alleviate his frustrations. Many previous texts had race as a factor, but Wright foregrounds racial oppression so much that every page of the novel echoes Bigger's sense of exclusion. Hints of interracial interactions between Black males and white females were minimized and offstage in previous texts, whereas Wright makes Bigger and Mary the centerpiece of *Native Son*. Interracial sexual dynamics are lifted to the surface in ways that no ancestor to *Native Son* had done. Race, sex, and transgression combine in an explosive, unforgettable brew that makes the novel an exception to many expected arenas of presentation. Thus, Bigger's literary forebears are few, and they differ in intent and focus. Take, for example, Sutton E. Griggs's *Imperium in Imperio* (1899), in which Belton Piedmont and Bernard Belgrave both want to transform America, though Belgrave envisions a violent overtaking of the state of Texas where the Imperium, the secret society of Black males fighting segregation, is located. In Charles W. Chesnutt's *The Marrow of Tradition* (1901), Josh Green becomes a martyr by ignoring the effects of a direct hit from a bullet in order to stab to death the white man whom he has witnessed murder his father years earlier.[15]

Imperium in Imperio, which Griggs self-published (a significant fact given the pressures of publishing that Black writers faced in the nineteenth and early twentieth centuries) and which was not generally known until it was reissued by West Virginia University Press in 2003, features strong African American males with visions of self-determination. They may be wrongheaded in their aspirations, and they may turn against each other, but they nonetheless dream. By contrast, Bigger might resort to the kind of violence they advocate, but it is misdirected in that it grows out of fear of discovery with Mary and fear of capture with Bessie; the only thing that approaches a dream that Bigger has is his desire to fly planes, despite his lack of preparation in becoming a pilot. Bigger does not see the value of school (indeed, he has dropped out), and he fails to make the connection between his thoughts and his actions. At no point does Bigger associate school-based learning with success in life. He is skeptical about his sister Vera's taking courses in sewing at the local Y.W.C.A., and he never suggests to his brother Buddy that he can achieve anything through attending school. Lack of vision, then, is one of the things that separates Bigger from these literary antecedents.

Chesnutt's Josh Green, again unlike Bigger, has a purpose. He knows, as Bigger does, that he is oppressed, but he directs constructive effort toward ending that oppression. Having identified the racist Captain McBane as the epitome of his oppression, Josh moves in a direct—and manly, by traditional standards—way to bring about change. On the other hand, Bigger strikes out at a weaker member of the society that oppresses him, and he does so accidentally, not deliberately. He is as shocked as readers are to learn that his holding the pillow over the face of Mary results in her death. He has resorted to such action out of fear (the title of this section of the book) and not with the purpose or determination that defines Josh Green, Belton Piedmont, or Bernard Belgrave. Bigger, then, in contrast to his Black male literary ancestors who defy white society and work to achieve something constructive, is basically without direction or purpose until after he kills Mary. Once he determines that she is indeed dead, he begins to act with an ill-informed plan when he burns her body, writes the ransom note, and delivers it to the front door of the Dalton home. He has not thought through his plan carefully or considered completely what escape route might be available to him. He is caught in circumstances that control him instead of his controlling them. Never is Bigger in control of much of anything, though I could certainly argue that his actions surrounding the disposal of Mary's body reflect some thought. By contrast, his killing Bessie and dumping her body down an airshaft with the money in her pocket that he has taken from Mary's purse illustrates the kind of short-sightedness that defines him for most of the text, for he has eliminated the financial resources that could have bought him possible escape from Chicago.

Griggs's male characters and Josh Green did not make the kind of shock waves in the literary world that Bigger did, and it is easy to imagine why. Griggs's characters direct their actions against a system of oppression, and Josh directs his against a local white supremacist. When Black males direct violent actions against white females, however, the proverbial feces hit the fan, and the splatter is earthshaking. Bigger thus executes the ultimate taboo, for not only has he touched a white woman, but he has killed her. And, as the racist district attorney Buckley will argue, he has also raped her. Given that accusations of rape of white women were the primary justification for the lynching of Black males in the United States, the assumed rape of Mary provides the justification for the legal lynching of Bigger. Bigger was thus born into a literary and a social/historical world where the actions of Black males were circumscribed, monitored, and always considered potentially dangerous. The added element of Mary gives Bigger and *Native Son* a more potent urgency than previous African American literary texts featuring Black males. Wright thereby achieves his purpose of creating a character who is too hard for bankers' daughters to cry over.

That hardness, while duplicated somewhat in other literary representations of Black male characters, does not reflect the majority of them. Readers and scholars need but contemplate the likes of Jimboy Rodgers in Langston Hughes's *Not Without Laughter* (1930) or Vergible "Tea Cake" Woods in Zora Neale Hurston's *Their Eyes Were Watching God* (1937) to view more acquiescent Black males whose primary concerns do not include undermining white society or the government at large. Indeed, in their folksiness and emphasis on blues music, Jimboy and Tea Cake border on stereotypes of the happy-go-lucky young Black male who leaves family and other kin for the sake of adventure, a figure that still appears years later in hit songs from the 1970s such as "Papa Was a Rollin' Stone" (by the Temptations) and "Living for the City" (Stevie Wonder).

The same lack of willingness to disturb the racial status quo also describes other novels that preceded *Native Son*, including such narratives of Paul Laurence Dunbar as *The Uncalled* (1898) and *The Sport of the Gods* (1902), as well as James Weldon Johnson's *The Autobiography of an Ex-Colored Man* (1927). The Dunbar novels portray characters whose circumstances may be defined by race, such as the Hamilton family patriarch in *The Sport of the Gods* being falsely imprisoned, but they carry on as best they can under those oppressive conditions. No anger motivates them, and they certainly do not perceive transforming society as within their purview. The Ex-Colored Man's love of music might be more sophisticated than Jimboy's or Tea Cake's, but it is nonetheless a pastime that does not upset the status quo. Indeed, Johnson's narrator buys solidly into the status quo when he becomes the trained musical pet of a world-traveling white millionaire. Novels such as Rudolph Fisher's *The Conjure-Man Dies* (1932) and Wallace Thurman's *The Blacker the Berry* (1929) take place primarily within African American communities. Fisher's is a detective novel while Thurman's illustrates the impact, in anticipation of Toni Morrison's *The Bluest Eye* (1970), of light-skinned beauty standards upon dark-skinned African American females. Claude McKay's continent-hopping Jake in *Home to Harlem* (1928) also exhibits concerns other than dismantling the status quo of white racism.

The literary world Bigger was born into, therefore, was rather tame in reference to any manner of racial disruption. Certainly novels before *Native Son* were progressions in character development from the nineteenth-century tragic mulatto representations, but some of them, such as Nella Larsen's *Quicksand* (1928) and *Passing* (1929), were still tainted with colorism or pigmentocracy, that pattern in African American communities in which persons of lighter skin coloring are valued more than those with darker pigmentation. More well-rounded depictions in the vein of vernacular representation, such as those in the tobacco factory sections of Johnson's *Autobiography of an Ex-Colored Man* or some sections of Thurman's *The Blacker the Berry,* and particularly those in Jean Toomer's *Cane* (1923), offer welcome contrasts to earlier literary portraits even if protest is not their primary driving force. Thurman,

Toomer, and Johnson ground their characters in situations that mostly do not evoke visceral reactions from their readers. Their characters go about their daily lives in ways that showcase Black existence but not as it grinds dramatically against what readers, especially white readers, might have expected. Bigger was something new in upsetting the usual.

Still . . . how might some of Bigger's older literary brothers and sisters have responded to their news-making baby brother's arrival? Josh in *The Marrow of Tradition* would have loved Bigger's anger; however, he would very quickly have learned that Bigger would not have been willing to join him in the riot that led to Captain McBane's death. Bigger is too frightened of direct confrontation with white people to envision such a frontal attack upon those he views as responsible for his oppression. During the time that he goes from one Chicago tenement to another to escape that mob of white policemen, Bigger reflects upon the discrepancies between Black and white lives and the economics of both, but those reflections do not—and have not previously, in Bigger's life—had a counterpart in action. What Bigger would have been willing to do is bar hop and whore in Harlem with his older brother Jake from McKay's *Home to Harlem*. Jake's carefree lifestyle would appeal to Bigger, because it has no tangible responsibility and little morality to guide it. Bigger would thus enjoy the drinking and the women without feeling the need to make definite commitments.

Bigger's older sisters in Larsen's novels, specifically Helga Crane in *Quicksand* and Irene Redfield in *Passing*, would simply be appalled at Bigger and his behavior. They, like Geraldine is later in Morrison's *The Bluest Eye*, are the keepers of early twentieth-century Black class divisions in the literature. Bigger represents everything they have escaped through education and, with Irene, through marriage. Irene could possibly hire Bigger's mother to take care of her children, but that is as close as she would come to the darker-skinned and lower-class Thomases. Since Helga teaches at the historically Black Naxos College, she might attempt to inspire Bigger to move toward education; however, since he has not managed to finish high school, her efforts would probably be wasted. And even though Helga's final position in the novel—married to a chocolate preacher, mired in an unhappy marriage, and pregnant with a fifth child in some tiny hovel in the Deep South—mirrors the economic fate of certain characters in *Native Son,* she is still, especially to some of the characters around her, superior to that status by virtue of her education and skin color.

For Helga and Irene, Wright perhaps captures their possible reactions to Bigger perfectly when he comments in "How 'Bigger' Was Born": "I knew from long and painful experience that the Negro middle and professional classes were the people of my own race who were more than others ashamed of Bigger and what he meant. Having narrowly escaped the Bigger Thomas reaction pattern themselves—indeed, still retaining traces of it within the confines of their own timid personalities—they would not relish being publicly reminded of the lowly, shameful depths of life above which they enjoyed their bourgeois lives. Never did they want people, especially *white* people, to think that their lives were so much touched by anything so dark and brutal as Bigger." Although he recognized that his creation of Bigger would probably meet resistance even within Black communities, Wright nonetheless persevered in his desire to bring the character to life and to publication. In his understanding of the significance of class, he chose to err, if others would view it that way, on the side of the working class.[16]

Wright credits his working at the Boys' Club on the South Side of Chicago as moving *Native Son* toward its final drafting. In that job, he was able to witness how the white power structure hoped to contain young Black males. The club, Wright notes, was "an institution which tried to reclaim the thousands of Negro Bigger Thomases from the dives and the alleys of the Black Belt." He continues: "Here, on a vast scale, I had an opportunity to observe Bigger in all of his moods, actions, haunts. Here I felt for the first time that the rich folk who were paying my wages did not really give a good goddamn about Bigger, that their kindness was prompted at bottom by a selfish motive. They were paying me to distract Bigger with ping-pong, checkers, swimming, marbles, and baseball in order that he might not roam the streets and harm the valuable white property which adjoined the Black Belt." Of course readers will recognize references that get incorporated into *Native Son*, for Mr. Dalton and others of his ilk are perfectly willing to support such distractions in order to contain young Black males whom they are not willing to embrace with opportunities for education and other forms of advancement. (Give Mrs. Dalton credit for allowing previous chauffeurs to go to school while they worked, although that means an education could take as long as ten years— or more. Also, one instance is barely measurable among the huge numbers of disgruntled young Black males who populate cities such as Chicago.)[17]

After mulling over approaches and possible reactions to the novel he had in mind, Wright took to the actual writing of *Native Son* with a great sense of relief. He had overcome the objections he imagined middle-class Black folks would offer as well as those he thought might come from Communist Party members. Wright had been at odds with the party for years about how his writing should best be developed and employed. His superiors wanted him to stifle individuality in favor of the party line of producing tracts and pamphlets, a position he rejected consistently. He had also overcome whatever objections and limitations he placed upon himself about his abilities to proceed with creating Bigger's life. The writing of the novel thus became, for him, "a necessity . . .

the writing of it turned into a way of living for [him]." The first
draft took only four months, which, given the reported length of
the narrative at 576 pages, suggests that Wright wrote at a fre-
netic, obsessive pace. A significant challenge, he asserts, was finding a way to begin the novel. He thus started with the pool hall
scene and only later, after a booze-induced night, during which
he remembered the many rats in Chicago tenements, did he come
up with the inspired opening scene and the cornered rat that has
become the epitome of how readers remember the novel.[18]

Once Wright transferred the narrative from his head to the
womb of pages before him, it was still several steps and some time
away from delivery to the general public. He spent several months
in 1938 and 1939 polishing the novel and getting reactions from
those closest to him physically and intellectually. He continued
to work on *Native Son* after he had delivered it to his editor on
June 11, 1939. He had the galleys in a month, because the Book-of-
the-Month Club wanted to use *Native Son* as its selection for September.[19] The final process of bringing *Native Son* to publication,
however, included a series of attendant midwives and some serious challenges. The Wright scholar Keneth Kinnamon agrees with
my use of birth and midwife imagery when he observes: "Wright's
novel was born, then, with the assistance of various white midwives,
male and female. However much domesticated by white assistance
at its delivery, it was still a robust infant whose loud cries rever-
berated through the literary atmosphere as the decade of the for-
ties began."[20]

Those attendant midwives who stood supportively with Wright
as he brought the novel to conclusion and put the polishing touches
on it were both white and Black. His editor, Edward Aswell, provided Wright with a publishing contract and a cash advance. Other
midwives included his friends Herbert and Jane Newton, whom
he lived with in various apartments in New York while he was

writing and revising the novel; his friend and fellow writer (play-wright) Theodore Ward, who shared living space in the same house as Wright at one point; his friend Ralph Ellison, whom Wright credits with having a crucial conversation that pushed him to reach the final page of the novel; his good friend Margaret Walker, who had collected several newspaper articles about a case in Chicago that informed Wright's portrayal of Bigger; and the group that Wright gathered to read the novel from beginning to end during the course of the evening of June 10, 1939.

The only reluctant midwife—and that only slightly so—was Wright's agent, Paul Reynolds, who, after reading *Native Son*, suggested that Wright make some changes in the novel, such as reconsidering whether the Daltons would trust their daughter to a new chauffeur or noting how few servants the wealthy Daltons had. Wright respected what his agent had to say, for he was certainly not unresponsive to criticism; however, he made only minor changes because he believed in his own vision for Bigger and the world into which he had placed him. Reynolds had also requested that Wright reconsider the length of Max's speech, which was one of the quibbles that the editor Aswell had as well. Wright biographer Hazel Rowley notes that Wright shortened the speech only minimally, to which Aswell responded: "As for the lawyer's speeches—well, you're the doctor and what you say goes." This was striking for the times, as Rowley explains: "Aswell's leniency was remarkable. Most publishing houses were reluctant to produce protest fiction, and they were not keen on Negro subject matter. Gene Saxton, the head of Harper & Brothers, had been reluctant to publish *Native Son*. As Aswell put it later, Saxton 'had a rule of thumb gained from his experience, that you can't publish successfully a book about Negroes, or by Negroes.' Aswell's enthusiasm for the book had carried the day."[21]

Reactions from Wright's editor and agent were minor inconveniences compared with the hindrances the Book-of-the-Month Club placed in Wright's path. After Aswell informed him that the most influential reading organization in the nation was considering selecting *Native Son* to recommend to its readers, it took ten months of back and forth communications and excisions and revisions before Wright produced a copy that the judges on the Selection Committee considered acceptable. A prominent member of the committee was Dorothy Canfield Fisher, a well-known white writer who later wrote the "Introduction" to the version of *Native Son* that circulated to Book-of-the-Month Club members.[22] Initially, the club insisted that Wright cut the scene in the theater in which Bigger and Jack masturbate. Then, they wanted changes to ensure that Mary was not perceived as a morally loose white woman. Instead of her responding to Bigger as she is aroused during the scene in her bedroom, she is transformed into an inert object upon whom the sexually uncontrollable Black male brute acts. Wright's biographer Rowley sums up the changes in the scene in which Mary grinds her body against Bigger's: "In this passage, Mary suddenly makes movements that are not limp at all. Wright intended every detail of her thrusts and grinds. The judges had the white woman's hips stilled. Mary became passive, limp as a rag doll, scarcely conscious. Bigger became the archetypal black beast pawing the sleeping beauty. The white woman was completely absolved from responsibility."[23]

In considering such changes, and with Fisher taking the lead role in imposing them, it is not far-fetched to compare her role in relation to Wright with that of Mary in relation to Bigger. Each instance involves a white woman's attempt to impose her vision upon a Black male. Mary is confident that her way of seeing the world, with unions working for victimized proletarians such as Bigger, is the "right" way to view socioeconomic conditions and the status of Black people in America. If only she could pour her ideas into Bigger's head, then surely Bigger would see the world as she does. Fisher was equally confident that the readers of the Book-of-the-Month Club would want the changes that she urged Wright to make. She emerges as a keeper of morality and all things pristine; the "dirty" Bigger and his friends cannot be allowed to pollute the minds of the club's readership. Readers will never know what would have happened if *Native Son* had been published *exactly* as Wright wrote it, but we do know the role that Fisher played in ensuring that it was not.

Scholars might wonder, as Rowley does: "Why did Wright consent to changes that made Bigger look like a potential black rapist? Did he argue? Did he give in easily? We don't know. But the fact is, he gave in to white pressure. By September 1939, his novel was no longer the same book that had crossed the judges' desk that summer. Bigger looked more guilty; the white woman was back on her traditional pedestal as the inaccessible object of desire." Some of the answers to those questions are tied to Wright's ambition, to an almost desperate desire to give birth to a novel and continue to move up in the literary circles where Wright had already gained a reputation as a poet, short fiction writer, and essayist. After years of working on novels and having circulated two previous ones to publishers without either one being accepted, Wright commented to several friends that he did not think *Native Son* would be published. Having come so close, therefore, is one possible explanation for his agreeing to the changes and allowing the novel to proceed to publication. On the other hand, Arnold Rampersad, who worked with the Library of America to restore the original version of the novel, has a simple response to the question of why: "Poor all of his life and eager for a financial windfall, Wright assented" to the changes.[24]

Thus Bigger Thomas, with some slightly reluctant supporters and the blessings of all those close to Wright who had a hand in his creation and delivery, made his entry into a world that proved, alternately, to be nurturing, un-nurturing, and downright confounding. Of most significance is that Richard Wright gave to the world a character never seen or perhaps even envisioned before: an angry young Black man who defies social custom and breaks crucial laws, a young Black man who goes to his death unrepentant about his actions and who appears as foreign to his attorney as the creation of the novel might have appeared to some readers. Bigger announced to the world that now that he was out of the womb, who he was and what he represented could never be sent back to oblivion. The world would need to deal with him even as he dealt with the world that he was forced to call home. Bigger therefore made history even as he evoked history.

CHAPTER 2

———

Of Men and Monsters

EVEN THE BRIEFEST PERUSAL of Richard Wright's non-fiction will reveal the extent to which he saw the intimate connections, historical and contemporary, between African American life and culture and creative depictions of that history and culture. That history includes a pattern of demonizing Black males, thingafying them, labeling them subhuman monsters. In *Native Son*, Wright mediates such potential-denying and life-threatening perceptions. For Wright, literature has an activist function, and that function is to improve the lives of African-descended people living on United States soil. He makes his position clear in "Blueprint for Negro Writing," an essay he composed after moving to New York from Chicago to assume editing duties for a recently established little magazine, *New Challenge*. The Communists he associated with insisted on subsuming the plights of American Negroes under the broad strokes of worldwide class struggle, but Wright believed Marxism could only be a starting point for Black writers, not their ultimate destination. He was adamant about retaining the nationalist, racial dynamic at the core of interracial relations in America, which, rooted in slavery and the liberty-restricting codes that white supremacists legislated after slavery, ensured that African-descended people would always be second-class citizens. Bigger feels these exclusions intensely.

Wright therefore asserts in "Blueprint for Negro Writing" that history is the basis for African American creativity, and he cites the impactful nature of Black churches and the Black folk tradition as key components. That he uses "Blueprint" in the title shows his expectation that his offerings will serve as a guide not only to himself but to other African American writers. Wright posits: "Theme for Negro writers will emerge when they have begun to feel the meaning of the history of their race as though they in one life time had lived it themselves throughout all the long centuries." Although he argued that literature should not be a carbon copy of life, he also highlighted the cultural work that it can do: "Negro writers should seek through the medium of their craft to play as meaningful a role in the affairs of men as do other professionals."[1]

Wright was thinking and writing this in 1938, long before African American writers were given—and felt—the right to create whatever they wanted to create. Although he stated that, "if the sensory vehicle of imaginative writing is required to carry too great a load of didactic material, the artistic sense is submerged," and claimed that writing has its "professional autonomy," there are still countless autonomy-free values that he carries into his writing. For example, he wrote the essay at the request of senior members of the Communist Party, and he was certainly influenced by their concerns; still, he was also obviously attuned to the contemporary state of American social, political, and racial affairs. At this point, the country was rife with bigotry, the new slavery in the form of sharecropping, and lynching as a form of punishment for perceived Black transgressions. Wright thus joined other African

American cultural thinkers and writers in advocating that literature African Americans produce *must* have a social function in
addition to its literary function.[2]

From Wright's perspective, previous African American writers
had not stood "shoulder to shoulder" with the Black masses, a
position that he argued was absolutely critical; instead, those earlier writers had pursued more individualistic writing objectives.
In advocating for a social function in art, Wright presented thoughts
that are an intensification of those of W. E. B. Du Bois, who, a few
years earlier, asserted, "all Art is propaganda and ever must be,
despite the wailing of the purists. I stand in utter shamelessness
and say that whatever art I have for writing has been used always
for propaganda for gaining the right of black folk to love and
enjoy. I do not care a damn for any art that is not used for propaganda." Wright also echoed the famed poet and editor James Weldon Johnson, who claimed: "The final measure of the greatness
of all peoples is the amount and standard of the literature and art
they have produced. The world does not know that a people is
great until that people produces great literature and art." Du Bois
shared a similar sentiment when he asserted that "until the art of the
black folk compels recognition they will not be rated as human."[3]

Johnson therefore encouraged Black writers to move beyond
dialect as a form of capturing working-class Black life and experience and into something more comparable in creative range to
"what Synge did for the Irish." Both Du Bois and Johnson were
aware of the watchful gaze whites directed toward African Americans, a gaze that could sometimes be friendly but was much more
often critical or dismissive, if not downright hostile. Johnson aimed
his comments to white observers, directing them to be more toler-
ant with that gaze, which meant that he consistently emphasized
the close affiliation between Black life and Black art. He concluded
that the sooner Black American poets learned how "to write *Amer-*

ican poetry spontaneously, the better"; realism, he believed, would simultaneously advance acceptance of Black people into the larger society even as it revealed the struggles and issues that defined African American communities. Johnson was perhaps a bit less insistent on the ties between art and life that guided Wright, but he serves well as one of Wright's literary and theoretical ancestors.[4]

Du Bois and Johnson, predecessors of Wright, understood as well as he did the power of literature not only to transform the larger world's perception of a given group, but also the need to fight against white oppression by any means available. Du Bois was a founding member of the National Association for the Advancement of Colored People (NAACP), and both he and Johnson spent many years teaching in historically Black colleges and universities in an effort to pass on wisdom and strategies to continue the fights against discrimination.

In the first third of the twentieth century, therefore, literature was certainly viewed as a reflection of the truth of life. A short and vivid example is a poem, "Incident," by Countee Cullen, a contemporary of Du Bois, Johnson, and Wright. It recounts the brief narrative of an eight-year-old Black boy who visits Baltimore, sees a young white boy looking at him, attempts with a smile to befriend the child, and has his gesture dramatically rejected when the young white boy "poked out/ His tongue and called" the speaker "nigger." The speaker concludes: "I saw the whole of Baltimore/ From May until December;/ Of all the things that happened there/ That's all that I remember." If racism operates so vividly on this small scale, at this level of innocence, then how much more relevant is it when a Black adult male is accused of improper behavior with a white woman, as with Bigger? For Wright, there could be little separation between the lives he knew African Americans lived and the literature he wanted to create about those lives.[5]

The American racial history that guided Wright's creative

energies evolved into the circumstances that led to composing *Native Son* and limning Bigger. What kind of world, then, did young Black males like Bigger find themselves in during the first four decades of the twentieth century? In what ways does Bigger reflect them and their circumstances, and in what ways do they echo Bigger?

According to the historian John Hope Franklin, living conditions for Black people in the first few decades of the twentieth century had not changed appreciably from what they had experienced in the latter decades of the nineteenth century. Social and political circumstances post-slavery, as well as custom, ensured that Black people would not move toward equality in the society. During the Depression era, just before Bigger was born, "the bulk of African Americans that found employment fell into the unskilled and semiskilled categories where there was little or no union organization." When African Americans did work in occupations with union representation, Franklin notes, they were often forced to join separate locals. Wright's awareness of workers' plights thus made Communism even more attractive to him, even with its limitations. Wright managed to find a job in a post office, but his offspring Bigger would probably have been limited to garbage collecting, street sweeping, or any other job where physical labor mattered more than mind work.[6]

Restrictive Black codes of the late nineteenth century gave way to the convict lease system and sharecropping as new forms of slavery in the twentieth century. As Douglas A. Blackmon documents in *Slavery by Another Name* (2008), any Black male could be picked up from the streets of any town or city, especially in the South, jailed for vagrancy, and hired out or sold to local white landowners who needed workers, usually in very physically demanding jobs such as farming or mining. If Bigger and his friends had dared to hang out in Birmingham, Alabama, for example, they could easily have been scooped up, arrested, imprisoned, and sold to nearby farmers, where they most likely would have been worked to death. Blackmon notes that young Black males in southern states, particularly the Alabama territory on which he focuses, could also be reenslaved in more dramatic ways when unscrupulous white racists simply kidnapped them and locked them away for work. Blackmon recounts several instances of such capture and reenslavement, where Black males were chained underground to work in coal mines or shackled in sheds to work on isolated farms. The inability of these men to control their fates is just as poignant as with Bigger in his restlessness and inability to locate a space and a place in American society that will enable him to realize his full potential. Awareness of these life-altering practices serves as a guiding force in Wright's portrayal of Bigger.[7]

Black males not pressed into illegal labor found jobs available to them almost as restrictive as those forced upon their impressed counterparts. According to the United States Bureau of Labor Statistics, in 1940, "two thirds of all employed Negroes worked" in "agriculture . . . and the service industries." That means that the majority of Black males in the United States were confined to jobs that called for grueling, backbreaking physical labor, whether it was farming, working in meat-packing factories in cities such as Chicago, hauling garbage, digging ditches and roads, or anything else that led to mental dullness quickly followed by physical deterioration. Mrs. Thomas is insistent that Bigger get a job, but her conception of what a job means for a young Black man in 1940 can only align with what is available, and most of what is available involves harsh physical labor. Bigger, in his role as a chauffeur, is granted a better job than the average Black male was historically. Bigger is certainly more appreciative of his job than Walter Lee Younger is in Lorraine Hansberry's *A Raisin in the Sun* (1959), who tells his mother when she asserts that his chauffeur job is a good one: "Mama, that ain't no kind of job . . . that ain't nothing at all." Since Walter Lee and Bigger want to achieve the impossible without preparation for it (Walter wants to own a successful business without a hint of a business plan or startup funds, and Bigger wants to fly planes without ever having taken a class), they are both caught in the trap of short-circuited expectations and dreams turned into nightmares that many Black American males experienced historically.[8]

How, then, could Black males—and Black people generally—who felt such restrictions so keenly try to work around them? Attempting to escape racial confinement and the limitations that accompanied it provided motivation for the Great Migration, that mass movement of Black people in the first several decades of the twentieth century from the Deep South into northern cities such as Detroit, Chicago, New York, and Buffalo, and western cities such as Los Angeles. That is the path Bigger's family has taken, and so has the Younger family in Hansberry's play. When Walter Lee Younger recounts that his family comprises five generations of sharecroppers, he is reflecting southern reality that led to northern migration toward what Black migrants hoped would be better conditions.

Wright joined fictional and historical counterparts in the desire for better opportunities up north. At the end of his autobiography, *Black Boy* (1945), Wright recognizes that, even as he is leaving Memphis for Chicago, he is also taking a part of the South with him. Yet, he is hopeful: "I was taking a part of the South to transplant in alien soil, to see if it could grow differently, if it could drink of new and cool rains, bend in strange winds, respond to the warmth of other suns, and, perhaps, to bloom."[9] Wright echoes the desires of many Black Southerners of all ages and work experiences who arrived in the North with incredible hope and soon discovered that their dreams had to be deferred yet again. Living conditions, job and educational opportunities, and possibilities for social advancement were frequently as limited in the North as in the South. Hope fought reality as migrants from southern states continued to pour into northern cities. They were subjected to overcrowded, overpriced, dilapidated housing; undesirable even if decent-paying jobs; lack of choice in living spaces; swindles and other crimes; and raging communicable diseases, such as tuberculosis. Government photographs from the period, medical records, and a host of other documents mark how much migrants endured in their hopeful entries into the North. Wright joined that documentation with his publication of *12 Million Black Voices: A Folk History of the Negro in the United States* (1941), a photographic and essayistic depiction of the conditions under which southern migrants lived in cities such as Chicago.[10]

Physical confinement in the North equated in many ways to social confinement in the South. Blacks in the South worked closely with whites on farms and in homes and often lived nearby, but physical restrictions in the North redlined them into designated living areas, which usually amounted to the most undesirable territories, such as near elevated trains and other railroad tracks, next to stockyards, or far away from public transportation. Maps of Chicago and other northern cities show clearly how these patterns were enforced in the first half of the twentieth century. Restrictive housing covenants took over where physical limitations ended to keep people of African descent in Chicago—and throughout the United States—contained and controlled. Yet, even as Black people—and especially Black men—were confined economically, socially, physically, and in every other way imaginable, they were viewed as a constant threat to the larger society.

That threat was usually imagined as criminal activity of one sort or another. Indeed, the narrative about the criminality of Black males served as a direct impetus to violent repression. Black males were not considered capable of rising up, leading revolutions, and overthrowing the government, but they were viewed as threats with an imagined potential to wreak havoc against white bodies and property. Such attitudes, as Blackmon shows, are carryovers from slavery and late-nineteenth-century efforts to kill the spirits and contain the minds of all Black people, but especially Black males. Bigger is therefore born into a world where his very physical self is suspect and threatening, and his brothers historically know that suspicion does not need much motivation to transform into the larger society's version of truth.

With history as the backdrop against which his actions are viewed, Bigger finds himself caught in the ultimate criminal activity that white society viewed Black males as being capable of: the presumed raping and killing of a white woman. Bigger violates multiple taboos as he marches toward the ultimate one: being in Mary Dalton's bedroom and smothering her to death. Unfortunate circumstances combined with accidental guilt ensure that Bigger will reap the whirlwind of condemnation and violence that historical Black male victims reaped. Buckley's claims against Bigger for his killing—and presumed raping—of Mary evoke comparison to nineteenth-century depictions of the Negro as a "beast"; recall the numerous instances in *Native Son* in which characters, from Buckley to newspaper editors or reporters, use bestial descriptions in their references to Bigger. Consider as well that, when the Ku Klux Klan was formed in the latter part of the nineteenth century, one of its ostensible purposes was to protect white life (especially white females) and property, particularly from presumably vicious and violent Black males. Implicit criminality was also assigned to Black males in D. W. Griffiths's film *The Birth of a Nation* (1915), which fired the popular imagination as assuredly as newspaper accounts of Bigger's killing of Mary sparked such negative imaginings in the minds of whites in Wright's novel.

According to this narrative, Black males found in the presence of white females when those white females are harmed are already guilty of whatever the public imagination ascribes to them. With the very weather arrayed against him (which literally becomes the case when the snow and ice finally prevent his additional movement as the mob catches up with him), Bigger cannot escape the history that precedes his birth or the history that will watch over his demise. He undergoes, therefore, a legal lynching.

As the historian Robert L. Zangrando notes, "whites created the myth that lynching was a necessary protection for white womanhood."[11] Zangrando joins other historians in noting that lynchings for rape accounted for one fourth to one third of the total numbers of lynching, yet, as I point out in my study of literary lynchings, an accusation of rape against a white woman by a Black male was the lock-step, guaranteed emotional response that yielded, without question, a call for lynching.[12] Black people could be "lynched for such transgressions of racial mores as sheltering a fugitive, disputing a white man's word, dating a white woman, testifying or defending themselves against whites," and for "daring to look at or speak to a white person, wearing fancy clothes, having too much education, slapping a white person, or killing a white person," but an assumption of rape met automatic mob violence and brutal execution.[13] There were no extenuating circumstances to consider, just as Bigger will find that there is nothing—absolutely *nothing*—that he or his Communist attorney Max can do to deter his fate.

Bigger commits a series of lynchable offenses, the first of which is his *touching* Mary Dalton's white female body. She may be drunk, and she may need help, but Bigger's touching of her is taboo. Fortunately for him, at this point in the narrative there are no witnesses, and Mary is too inebriated to offer any testimony against him even if she were inclined to do so. Another offense that could lead to lynching is his entry into portions of the Dalton mansion beyond the kitchen, his room, and the basement, all spaces to which Bigger has been given explicit access. He furthers the violation by moving into the hallway of the mansion and on to Mary's bedroom. Daring to enter Mary's bedroom is far, far beyond what any white person is willing to tolerate. Again, it does not matter that Mary needs help, that she is in a pathetic drunken state; Bigger will be viewed as the violator. Think about how the society in Alabama responds so vehemently to Tom Robinson in Harper Lee's *To Kill a Mockingbird* (1960) when he testifies that he felt sorry for the young, white-trash girl who has accused him of rape when she invited him into her home.[14] A Black male cannot bestow such consideration upon a white female, no matter her socioeconomic status. Thus the post-event "witnesses" to Bigger's entrance into Mary's bedroom can attribute whatever motives and actions to him they desire. Rape and killing, whether accidental or not, whether committed or not, seal a Black male's fate in connection to a white female.

Another crucial step in sealing his fate is to paint Bigger as a monster loosed upon the innocence of white women. That begins with newspaper accounts of what has happened to Mary and ends with Buckley's uncensored remarks in the courtroom. Buckley's comments solidify the perception—undergirded many times historically with fact—that "justice" can never be applied fairly, untaintedly, to Black male defendants. The *Chicago Tribune*, in its description of Bigger, provides the fuel that many of its readers can use to justify the legal lynching. "He looks exactly like an ape!" it records from one "terrified young white girl," then paints Bigger with these strokes of monstrosity.

> His lower jaw protrudes obnoxiously, reminding one of a jungle beast. . . . All in all, he seems a beast utterly untouched by the softening influences of modern civilization. . . .

The moment the killer made his appearance at the inquest, there
were shouts of "Lynch 'im! Kill 'im!"

But the brutish Negro seemed indifferent to his fate. . . . He acted
like an earlier missing link in the human species. He seemed out of
place in a white man's civilization.[15]

The article quotes a white Southerner who asserts that, had Bigger been in Dixie, "no power under Heaven could have saved him
from death at the hands of indignant citizens." The fictional newspaper account joins those historically that stirred up masses to at-
tend lynchings and even printed days and times when lynchings
were scheduled. The article also makes clear that a southern mentality of dealing with instances of Black violations of white injunc-
tions has migrated north along with the bodies of Black people.[16]

The use of the word "civilization" as the exclusive purview of
white Americans is also relevant here, for it captures precisely the
insider/outsider, lack of citizenship status that defined African-
descended people at this point in American history. Bigger is a
thing that has crept onto the soil, into the homes, and now, by his
violation, into the imaginations of white Americans. He is not only
a stepson, a *non*-native son, but he is a veritable outsider, a monster intent on destroying the very foundations of the country and
what its white citizens hold dear: white families and white women.
The foreignness that Bigger represents, which is rooted in the human
versus the nonhuman, places him outside human sympathy, outside human mercy, and outside the safeguards of American justice.[17]
By his action, according to this logic, Bigger is expendable, and the
most expedient way of dispensing with him is to blot him from
the society, thus echoing the desire Bigger has to blot out people
and things that hurt him to his core and about which he can do
nothing. By contrast, the white citizens at his "trial" do have the
power to eliminate him.

What the newspaper account puts forth prepares readers for Buckley's attack on Bigger and Buckley's reiteration of the assumption that Bigger is beyond *any* human consideration. What Bigger has been judged to have done is so vile, so *un*civilized, according to Buckley, that total obliteration of the offender is the only possible response. With public opinion on his side and with local citizens having embraced thoroughly the popular narrative of Black male criminality, Buckley feels confident in referring to Bigger as a raging, uncontrollable beast. He labels Bigger "utterly beast-like and foreign to our whole concept of life" (with "our" again indicating the exclusion of African-descended people from American society); "black ape," "a bestial monstrosity"; "this black lizard," "this black mad dog," "this subhuman killer"; "this hardened black thing," "this rapacious beast"; "this beast"; "this black cur," "that maddened ape!" "That treacherous beast"; "a coiled rattler!" "this worthless ape"; and "this demented savage." With these constant references during his concluding speech at Bigger's trial, Buckley may well be a cheerleader for lynching, one who sends a fellow mobster for the rope that the original crowd might have been too hasty to bring or for the oil that was inadvertently forgotten in the excitement of anticipating viewing a man burn to death. Huge crowds listening outside the courtroom hear and pass along Buckley's expressed sentiments.[18]

Although Buckley paints him as bestial, dumb, stupid, and illiterate, Bigger understands perfectly what the emotional registers of the inquest and the trial are designed to accomplish. When Buckley orders Bessie's murdered and mutilated body brought into the inquest, it is not out of consideration for a Black woman who has met her untimely death in such a violent fashion. The move is designed only to highlight Bigger's so-called monstrosity. Indeed, Buckley rapes and kills Bessie a second time by not giving a damn about the lack of dignity and disrespect inherent in his publicly exposing her nude body. Bigger understands as well that the exposure is to show the extent of his inhumanity and monstrosity, for the narrator notes Bigger's reaction: "He understood what was being done. To offer the dead body of Bessie as evidence and proof that he had murdered Mary would make him appear a monster; it would stir up more hate against him." And indeed it does. If Bigger is so monstrous that he has done this to a woman of his own race, then imagination can only fill in the blanks about what he would have been willing and must have done to the white Mary. Bessie is expendable, but Mary is sacrosanct. That contrast is sufficient enough, so those immersed in the narrative of Black male criminality would conclude, to send Bigger to the outer reaches of hell.[19]

What Buckley fails to consider, and what history could not accomplish in its national failure to pass an antilynching bill, is that killing is not erasure. And that is where Bigger stands against the legal and extralegal white mobs that want to make him disappear from the society that they believe belongs exclusively to them. Bigger has been born into a racist society that would prefer that he not exist. Yet, despite their best efforts at confinement in terms of education, employment, and other life possibilities, Bigger exists and, as Wright hoped he would, challenges the society's treatment of Black males. Killing hundreds of Biggers simply means that thousands pop up. Suppressing thousands simply means that hundreds of thousands will approach the door to democracy yet again and ask—politely if possible, urgently if not—that it be opened to them. As Claude McKay asserts in his poem "The White House," the door may be shut against his "tightened face," a face that keeps asking for admittance to equitable treatment, but he will never give up the fight. He will bear his anger "proudly and unbent" and will strive to keep his "heart inviolate/ Against the potent poison" of the "hate" that is directed toward him.[20] Wright did not give up,

and Bigger has persisted in claiming the imaginations of generations of readers who recognize the limiting American conditions
he was born into and who have worked diligently for decades to
bring about changes to them. Ultimately, Bigger is the character
who earns sympathy, and Buckley seems a throwback racist who
uses the legal system to further his personal agenda. He is arguably more monstrous than Bigger.[21]

The times and the impunity with which Buckley operates
highlight yet again how art can have a social function. Even more
is this the case when we consider a historical event that was occurring in Chicago as Wright was in the final stages of bringing
Bigger to the public, the case of Robert Nixon. Since Wright moved
to New York, the Black novelist and poet Margaret Walker kept him
informed throughout 1938 on the case in Chicago, and he incorporated some of the details into *Native Son*. Nixon was a young
Black man accused of killing several white women, including a
mother and her twelve-year-old daughter, with bricks in 1937 and
1938. He was dubbed "The Brick Moron" because, though he was
believed to be a vicious killer, he appeared to be dimwitted (he
was smart enough to use several aliases during that two-year period). He moved between Los Angeles and Chicago, with murders
occurring in both cities. Nixon confessed to four of the murders,
was tried, and was executed on June 16, 1939, at the age of nineteen. As the case unfolded, Wright requested that Walker send him
newspaper articles about it, which she said "began an activity that
lasted a year, sending Wright every clipping published in the Chicago newspapers on the Nixon case." As with Bigger, the newspaper accounts of Nixon's deeds were unrelentingly racist. Walker
recalls that "there were times when the clippings were so lurid I
recoiled from the headlines."[22]

One headline in particular warrants attention. "Brick Slayer
Is Likened to Jungle Beast," by Charles Leavelle, appeared in the

Chicago Daily Tribune on June 5, 1938. Like Bigger, Nixon is taken to the scene of one of his crimes and asked to reenact it. (Nixon acquiesces; Bigger does not.) As Nixon climbs the fire escape to get to the apartment of the woman he is reputed to have raped and murdered, Leavelle notes this dehumanizing comment from one policemen: "Look at him go, . . . Just like an ape." Leavelle's own position merges with that of the mob gathering to witness the scene, and it becomes clear that he agrees with the dehumanization. After noting that Nixon has "none of the charm of speech or manner that is characteristic of so many southern darkies," Leavelle writes: "That charm is a mark of civilization, and so far as manner and appearance go, civilization has left Nixon practically untouched. His hunched shoulders and long, sinewy arms that dangle almost to his knees; his outthrust head and catlike tread all suggest the animal. He is very black—almost pure Negro. His physical characteristics suggest an earlier link in the species." There are noticeable echoes of the civilized being contrasted to the savage, of Blackness being equated to lack of humanity, just as Wright portrays in Buckley's remarks as well as in the fictional—or not so fictional—newspaper accounts. Indeed, in "How 'Bigger' Was Born," Wright explicitly noted the influence of the Nixon case to his creativity: "when I was halfway through the first draft of *Native Son* a case paralleling Bigger's flared forth in the newspapers of Chicago. (Many of the newspaper items and some of the incidents in *Native Son* are but fictionalized versions of the Robert Nixon case and rewrites of news stories from the *Chicago Tribune*.)"[23]

In the *Tribune* article in *Native Son,* a southern sheriff offers commentary on how white Southerners would deal with Bigger. When the sheriff in Nixon's hometown of Tallulah, Louisiana, is contacted, he comments that Nixon was a thief and "on the prowl since he was 6. . . . It has been demonstrated here that nothing can be done with Robert Nixon. Only death can cure him." That an adult officer of the law would describe a six-year-old as being "on the prowl" not only attributes animalistic characteristics to the child but illustrates how, no matter how young a Black male on American soil might be, he is not exempt from racial condemnation. Similarly, shouts of "Lynch him! Kill him!" hurled at Bigger are direct quotations from Leavelle's article. They reflect the mob mentality that Wright captures so vividly in *Native Son*. Accusations of rape—either committed or assumed—also link the historical case to the fictional one. Art and life continue to reflect each other, therefore, in poignant ways that enabled Wright to have Bigger resonate with the world he was born into and clamor loudly for redress of the conditions that shaped his birth and the severely cramped life he was forced to lead.

CHAPTER 3

———

Lightning in a Bottle

W HEN *NATIVE SON* reached bookstores on March 1, 1940, copies flew off the shelves: the novel sold two hundred and fifty thousand copies in the first six weeks. Practically everybody who was anybody in the Black reviewing world (Ralph Ellison, Alain Locke, Langston Hughes), in the white reviewing world (David Cohn, Burton Rascoe), in the Communist Party (Benjamin Davis, Jr., Mike Gold), and in various academic communities (Sterling A. Brown, Alain Locke) weighed in.[1]

There were, first, detractors who felt it necessary to convey to the white reading public that Bigger did not represent Black males generally and that the events in the novel are not uniquely characteristic of Black people. Then there were readers such as Margaret Walker, who, though she had provided Wright with many of the sources he used in *Native Son*, felt confounded and puzzled by how he had portrayed Bigger and his interactions with Mary and Bessie. Supporters, however, won the day and were perhaps best represented by the well-known white writer Dorothy Canfield Fisher, who wrote the Introduction to the version of *Native Son* selected for the Book-of-the-Month Club. The book began its tenure as a club selection in March 1940. It also spent almost fifteen weeks on best-seller lists. Thus Bigger, the defiant, violent young Black man who shocked so many readers, was transformed into a darling of the literary world and the stage of the early 1940s, for audiences both Black and white. Bigger was a jolt to the African American literary nervous system, an unapologetic and uncompromising blight on any sense of middle-classness and "best foot forward" representation characteristic of some of the earlier literary depictions of Black males.

Since Wright had intentionally taken the maligned "individualistic" approach to writing that most Communists despised, what Communists thought about the novel led observers—and Wright—to watch carefully for their responses, even though, as his biographer Michel Fabre notes, he did not expect praise from party members. Davis, a prominent Black Communist who befriended Wright when he moved from Chicago to New York, completed an extended essay review that was not published until April 14, 1940. That noticeable delay might have meant something in itself. What was clear is that Davis had a measured and impressively thoughtful response to Wright's work, all from the perspective of Communist philosophy. What he gave in praise, however, he took back in criticism. Most praiseworthy to Davis was Wright's indictment of capitalism and the limitations it placed on persons such as Bigger. Davis labeled the novel "the most powerful and important novel of 1940." He then proceeded to applaud—generously so—Wright's complaints against capitalism. "The book is a terrific indictment of capitalist America, which deliberately robs vast Negro communities and holds them in subjection in 'Southsides' and 'Harlems,' under appalling conditions of misery and discrimination, of childhood and adulthood without opportunity; of blockings of the main social highway and of forced detours to criminal by-ways. Bigger Thomas is the product of this special and bitter national oppression and, again and again, he finds himself caught in its web."[2]

As a successful, middle-class Black American turned Communist, however, Davis was not pleased that Wright did not separate out the masses of Blacks from the specific Bigger Thomas, which meant that readers, especially white readers, could easily conclude that all Negroes were like Bigger. "In fact one of the serious weaknesses of the book, particularly in the third part, is that the author overwrites Bigger into a symbol of the whole Negro people, a native son to the Negro people." Davis comments further: "It is true that Bigger symbolizes the plight of the Negro, but he does not symbolize the attitude of the entire Negro people toward that plight. Therefore, because no other character in the book portrays the Negro masses, the tendency becomes that the reader sees Bigger and no distinction whatever between him and the masses who are finding the correct way out despite capitalism. . . . In this case the failure of the book to bring forward clearly the psychology of the Negro mass will find the capitalist enemies of the Negro trying to attribute Bigger's attitude to the whole Negro people." To suggest that Wright was shortsighted or limited in his assessments of his own experiences could only raise his ire. His temperature probably rose even more when Davis suggested that most of Max's speech presented "distorted" and "confused" notions of Communism and should be "rejected." Even though, to reiterate Fabre's observation, Wright had not expected Communists to embrace *Native Son* unqualifiedly, he was nonetheless disappointed that one of the Black Communists whom he respected most was unwilling to see the overall worth of his work.[3]

Despite the Communist response, Wright still wanted readers to know and be as excited about his new creation as he was. He was like a proud father who had helped usher into the world his most cherished namesake, one who could establish him as a force in the literary world. As his biographer Constance Webb notes, Wright carried a copy of the book to his friend the playwright Theodore Ward, who lived in the same building in New York with Wright, and waited anxiously to hear his assessment. Ward did not disappoint: he concluded that reading *Native Son* was "the most amazing literary experience of [his] life." Wright was eager for good reviews and responded directly to reviewers whose assessments he found lacking. The proud father did not want his child maligned or misunderstood.[4]

A review that particularly riled the author appeared in the *Atlantic Monthly* in May 1940, in which David L. Cohn called Wright a liar, and asserted that he was historically ignorant and that, given the historical and contemporary gaps between Blacks and whites, Blacks can never reach a level of equity with white Americans. Cohn bypassed the art in *Native Son* to focus exclusively on the racial politics, which emphasizes yet again the close connections that Wright willfully made between history and literary creativity. Cohn began by claiming that Wright "has written a blinding and corrosive study in hate," because it represents Bigger as a symbol for the twelve million Blacks then residing in America. He asserted that if Wright had "stuck to fact," then he would know that Blacks outside the South "have complete political rights, including the suffrage" and that it is only in "the most benighted sections of the South" or "in times of passion arising from the committing of atrocious crime" that "the Negro" is denied "equal protection of the laws." Not only did Cohn deny Wright's reality, but he implicitly joined the very folks toward whom Wright directed *Native Son* in suggesting that Blacks commit crimes for which vicious and violent punishment is needed. In this way he echoed the southern sheriff who, in the novel, sent a message about how Bigger would have been treated if he resided in the South. Ultimately, Cohn concluded that "the Negro problem in America is actually insoluble," so Wright and other Blacks should be content "to make the best of the situation. . . . Justice or no justice, the whites of America simply will not grant to Negroes at this time those things that Mr. Wright demands."[5]

Seemingly unaware of his own racism, Cohn claimed that "the preaching of Negro hatred of whites by Mr. Wright is on a par with the preaching of white hatred of Negroes by the Ku Klux Klan." This claim by Cohn is as devoid of fact as he believed Wright's work to be, for there is no way that Blacks in 1940s America ever had narrative or literal power similar to that of the Ku Klux Klan. Cohn would probably have preferred that *Native Son* not reach bookstores, that Bigger had remained in the womb or at least arrived in the world stillborn. Unstated in Cohn's comments is an implicit "How dare he?"—a response that a member of the majority often expresses when a presumed subordinate complains about his or her subjugation. Cohn's condescending and at times lecturing tone (if Jews throughout the world waited two thousand years for redress of some of their grievances, Cohn argues, then why are Blacks in such a hurry?) evokes a visceral reaction even in the twenty-first century, so it must surely have done so in the mid-twentieth century.[6]

Cohn's blatant rejection and obvious distortion of what Wright had done, together with the explicit and implicit racism Cohn showed, left Wright so aggravated that he wrote a reply that appeared in the June issue of the *Atlantic Monthly*. Although the tone of Wright's reply was measured, he did include some exclamation-pointed parenthetical statements. Overall, he called attention to what Cohn had overlooked, dismissed, or distorted. Wright made two significant points. First, if the Jews have suffered, it is because they have not organized, formed alliances, and worked toward improving their situations. Wright thus toed the Communist Party line by highlighting the ties that Blacks in America were making "by joining in common cause with other oppressed groups (and there are a lot of them in America, Mr. Cohn!), workers, *sensible* Jews, farmers, declassed intellectuals, and so forth." Second, Wright turned the conversation to what Cohn had ignored: the purview of the artist. Artists can indeed take situations and judge them in an absolute sense, Wright avowed, which means that he retains the privilege of making Bigger a representative figure. Wright maintained that he did "not defend Bigger's actions; [he] explain[s] them through depiction." Certainly Bigger hates and fears whites, Wright noted, but the novel does not advocate hatred. Wright's comments probably did not change Cohn's mind, but they did showcase the mother-hen watchfulness Wright took toward responses to *Native Son* and the intensity of the bond he had with his literary son.[7]

Like Max in the novel, Cohn was perhaps a bit frightened to envision an America in which subordinates not only harbored thoughts of revenge but were ultimately unafraid to claim responsibility for those thoughts. To contemplate millions of Black Biggers who were dissatisfied with their status in American society and who might be willing to take change into their own hands rather than follow a more "respectable" path to assimilation shook Cohn and other middle-class whites to the core. Cohn's comments are thus a feeble attempt to contain and control any such possibility by reading *Native Son* and Bigger as assaults upon America rather than as a call to awakening America to its social and political inadequacies. Instead of moving toward correctives, Cohn attacked Wright and pushed back to the status quo. Cohn therefore worked hard in his review to paint Wright as an aberration if not a downright abomination. Implicit in Cohn's comments is a suggestion that Wright is somehow un-American simply for urging America to live up to its democratic promise and incorporate *all* Americans, Black and white, into that vision. Politically and aesthetically, therefore, Wright had broken out of the box into which the publishing world had locked most Black writers for decades.

Wright was equally riled by another negative review, and he responded to it as well. Burton Rascoe, writing in the May 1940 issue of the *American Mercury*, began by attacking reviewers who had praised Wright's novel by asserting that they had shown an "utterly juvenile confusion of values . . . in their ecstatic appraisal." Rascoe then quoted principles of fictional composition to which he believed Wright had failed to adhere, remarked on Wright's less than stellar speechmaking abilities (at a luncheon Rascoe attended), and suggested that Wright, by having been invited to speak to that gathering of white men, was "an embodied refutation of his theme in *Native Son*." When Wright noted that he hoped audience members would get a chance to meet Bigger, Rascoe claimed that he "shudders." He found the moral in *Native Son* to be "utterly loathsome and utterly insupportable as a 'message.'" He concluded finally that Bigger did not have "anything more to contend with, in childhood and youth, than I had or than dozens of my friends had," that "Bigger Thomas is just a small-scale Negro Hitler. Or a Negro Stalin or Mussolini," and that, if he had been on the jury, he would have voted "to hang Bigger." Rascoe, like Cohn, would have preferred that Bigger simply not reach the reading public. Readers can only imagine the ways in which such comments elevated Wright's blood pressure and led him to address the review head-on.[8]

Wright's response to Rascoe's review appeared in the June 1940 issue of the *American Mercury*. Wright questioned, first of all, how Rascoe's assessment of him as "a handsome young man" with a face that is "fine and intelligent" has anything to do "with the merits or shortcomings of a novel." He maintained that he would continue to write with the same intensity despite Rascoe's hope that he had gotten the subject matter of *Native Son* out of his system, and emphasized the value of writing from experience, re-affirmed his commitment to representing the lives of Black people, chastised Rascoe for distorting the remarks he made at the luncheon, and claimed autonomy "as an artist." He observed as well that Max's speech anticipated everything that Rascoe had said, for resistant readers unwilling to countenance the transformation of American society will elide guilt and attempt to justify the status quo.[9]

Wright obviously felt a need to respond to Rascoe, but he probably knew that his comments would not change Rascoe's mind. And indeed, they did not. Rascoe submitted his own response to the *American Mercury* in July 1940, mainly emphasizing Wright's Communist background and the whirlwind of terror Wright and other Blacks could reap if they listened to Communists enough to incite American whites to retaliate against them. The wide philosophical, political, and aesthetic chasm between Rascoe and Wright could not be bridged. Shaken by his contemplation of the uncertain future Bigger promised for America, Rascoe sought to hinder not only Bigger's literary life but Wright's creative one—perhaps as a way of hindering the future that Bigger augured. Indeed, Rascoe seemed to fit the situation as the scholar Jerry W. Ward, Jr., summed it up: "When [Wright's] second book, *Native Son*, was published in 1940, it was received as a rare first novel, a magic mirror which revealed as yet unexamined psychological monstrosities to the American public. Everyone who read it was forced to acknowledge the uncanny accuracy of Wright's vision or to become exceptionally defensive in retorting that such horrors as Wright described could not happen in America." Rascoe decidedly became defensive, and he joined Cohn in denying American racial reality, substituting it for the mythical constructs in his own mind.[10]

To readers such as Cohn and Rascoe, there are no innocent
Black males—and I deliberately use the word "males" because, as
noted earlier, some Black boys as young as six were believed to
be socially deviant. Just as Wright portrayed the consequences of
that lack of innocence in "Big Boy Leaves Home," so Cohn and
Rascoe maligned Bigger as the ugliest of monsters. Comparing a
young Black man in America to Hitler or Stalin or Mussolini casts
more aspersion on the person making such comparisons than it
does on Bigger. The total disregard of Black people's lack of political agency and power, lack of educational opportunities, and
lack of social equality illustrates the depths to which some reviewers were willing to go to blot Bigger from the American reading imagination (not unlike the repeated desire of Bigger to blot
out things and people who unsettle him). For Rascoe to assert that
he would vote to hang Bigger again illustrates the great gap between these reviewers, Bigger's life, and the circumstances in which
Wright placed his main character. Rascoe joins Cohn in providing
a sterling example of the lack of understanding of Black males
(and Black people generally) in America that Wright designed the
novel to address. Appropriately, their comments underscore the
social and literal blindness that serves as a major metaphor in
Native Son.

While Cohn and Rascoe would have preferred to be hinderers
to Bigger on his journey to literary immortality, their contemporary Dorothy Canfield Fisher was one of the helpers. That designation, however, was perhaps a mixed blessing. Certainly, the well-
known Fisher had significant influence in writing the Introduction
to *Native Son* for the Book-of-the-Month Club. The group's wide-
spread national reach and the selections it made assuredly had a
direct impact on the huge number of copies the novel sold. Founded
in 1926, the club moved from an initial circulation of 4,000 to
550,000 subscribers twenty years later. In 1939, the year before

Native Son appeared, the club had circulated 363,000 books. Although its membership waned in the early twenty-first century, it reached 100,000 in 2015, with 1.2 million Instagram followers. By instituting a book award and using social media, the club continues to be a powerful force in book sales and reading.[11]

Where the blessing of distribution became mixed with *Native Son,* however, was in Fisher's approach to introducing the novel. She took a cue from Wright—that he was placing Bigger in a laboratory to see how he would respond to various stimuli—and used the metaphor of a laboratory animal to the breaking point. She did not get specifically to *Native Son* until almost halfway through her two and a half pages of introduction. She began by referring to how "rats and other animals," including sheep, are trained to respond to one set of conditions, then placed in conditions where they cannot execute those responses. Nonetheless, they continue to try for the same results and thus develop neuroses that eventually lead to nervous breakdowns. What might generally be the case in the population at large is even more so with young Blacks: "But our society puts Negro youth in the situation of the animal in the psychological laboratory in which a neurosis is to be caused, by making it impossible for him to try to live up to those never-to-be-questioned national ideals, as other young Americans do." Fisher claimed that such experiments were known to the general public, but "*Native Son* is the first report in fiction we have had from those who succumb to these distracting cross-currents of contradictory nerve-impulses, from those whose behavior-patterns give evidence of the same bewildered, senseless tangle of abnormal nerve-reactions studied in animals by psychologists in laboratory experiments."[12]

This is an example of liberalism gone awry. In her effort to support Wright and his novel, Fisher ran the risk—as some reviewers did explicitly—of dehumanizing Bigger. The fact that she referred to the novel as a "report" supports this position, for it seems as if the author has merely observed and recorded instead of actually created a work of art. And Fisher's faint praise did not stop with the animal metaphor. She evoked Dostoevsky to compliment Wright on his "revelation of human misery in wrong-doing," then immediately equivocated, for she did "not at all mean to imply that *Native Son* as literature is comparable to the masterpieces of Dostoievski," except perhaps the last page when "the stultified Negro boy is born at last into humanity and makes his first simple, normal human response to a fellow-man." In the muddle of giving and taking back (as with Davis), Fisher could not bring herself to unqualifiedly compliment *Native Son*. Bigger is a lab animal; Wright is not comparable to Dostoevsky; and Wright has observed, rather than created. She also, perhaps inadvertently, equated Bigger and Wright.

It is difficult from the vantage point of the twenty-first century to see Fisher's comments as devoid of racism or condescension. In 1940, though, Wright was undoubtedly privileged to get this much of an endorsement from a prominent white literary figure. And she in turn probably thought she was being generous in her assessment without realizing how much she was denigrating both the author and his novel.

Fisher's reserved rather than robust Introduction underscores the position of Black writers in 1940s America who were dependent upon white evaluation and approval for their work. (Remember that Zora Neale Hurston did not want to write an autobiography, but her editor insisted, so she produced *Dust Tracks on a Road*, in 1942.) Wright was at the mercy of whites powerful enough to label *Native Son* and to control sales. The extent of that control is evident in the deletions to which Wright agreed to get his novel approved for the Book-of-the-Month Club.[13] His editor, Ed Aswell, accepted Fisher's Introduction *without* Wright having seen it, citing time pressures for his having done so. Not surprisingly, then, although Wright may have been grateful for the Introduction, he expressed only lukewarm thanks later.

Because Margaret Walker had played such a prominent role in providing supporting materials for Wright's portrayal of Bigger and the completion of *Native Son*, and because of her place in the "Chicago Renaissance" of Black literary life, her reaction warrants consideration. An issue surrounding her response, however, must be confronted head-on. Although what she thought about the novel cannot be challenged, she did not publish those thoughts until decades after she read *Native Son*. How time might have mitigated, intensified, or otherwise colored her reaction is left to readers to judge. What is important is that Walker responded at a wrenching gut level. She recounts that the "spectacular success of *Native Son* was unlike anything black or white America had seen of a black writer in the history of the country."[14] Still, she was "revolted" when she read the finished product. In her biography of Wright, she wrote:

I was in Iowa when I saw a copy of *Native Son* early in February 1940. I stayed in my room incommunicado and read it over and over for a week. I missed classes and kept my unpaid tuition check in my pocketbook. In spite of my contribution to *Native Son*, I was totally unprepared for the shock of the book. It rocked me on my heels. I asked myself half a dozen questions: 1. Why this negative treatment of Bessie? Of Bigger's mother? And the half-sister Vera? 2. Why such violence and brutality—all the psychosexual business of cutting off the Dalton girl's head and cramming her into the furnace, of raping Bessie and pushing her down a "big Black hole"? 3. How could an unconscious, illiterate boy like Bigger suddenly become conscious, literate, and articulate as in that last conversation with Max? 4. What is there in the criminal mind or subconscious that makes murder an

act of freedom? Emotional release and exhilaration are understandable, but not freedom. 5. Why is the cacophony of violence left naked
and unorchestrated? 6. Is the ending of the book contrived or revised?[15]

There is implicit in Walker's comment a feeling of betrayal, a
disruption to her very being as well as to her daily and professional activities. Underlying her reaction is an unstated assumption that, somehow, what Wright had done to Bigger amounted
to a violation of implied racial trust: why should Blacks need white
writers to malign and misrepresent them when they had one of
their own who eagerly accomplished that feat? Why would someone so literarily talented as Wright resort to such tactics of representation when he knew that the reading, literary world was
watching? Was he so eager for success and acceptance that he would
sacrifice writerly integrity? There might also have been a sense of
guilt that Walker felt for having supplied Wright with some of the
fuel to create this destructive fire. Her reaction was perhaps even
more acute given the fact that, by the time of the publication of
Native Son, her friendship with Wright had ended. Her visceral
reaction suggests the difficulty Walker had in processing what she
was reading. Her reaction might also have resulted partly from
Wright's treatment of Black women, a topic that had engaged Walker
and many others connected to Wright. In Wright's hands, therefore, Bigger could be slotted easily into the most vicious and monstrous Black "thing" that could be imagined in the United States,
independent of any creative fodder Wright might have offered.

Walker was an African American friend and intellectual who
responded to the book. Many other Black writers and intellectuals
also responded to the novel, as did general readers. As Fabre found,
"Black readers were often torn between their legitimate pride in
the literary fame of one of their own people and regret that he should
have destroyed their protective shield of respectability. The choice

of such an antisocial black protagonist, so near the bottom of the social ladder, was bound to confirm the racists' prejudice that the black man was a beast lusting after white women. The more enlightened understood, however, that the novel might bring at least the liberal whites to realize the gravity of the problem." Indeed, Walker might have felt some of that herself, since she was from a middle-class Black family with origins in Birmingham, Alabama, and New Orleans, Louisiana.[16]

Two other African American women, Lillian Johnson and Shirley Graham, shared contemporary negative reactions to *Native Son*. Johnson wrote a review that was published in the *Baltimore Afro-American*. Hers was one of the few negative reviews from African American readers, at least one of the few published ones. Johnson commented that Wright had failed to write "a book that will do anything constructive for his people as a race"; instead, it could "do a great deal of harm." She called attention to the absence of diversity in the Black characters Wright presented and wished that "the book had one intelligent colored person in it." Like Walker, Johnson was disturbed by the treatment of Bigger's relationship with Mary and wondered why the attraction was pictured as it was, with Bigger "desiring" Mary although "he did not like her."[17] Implicit in Johnson's comments is a middle-class perspective that inadvertently chastises Wright for not putting his "best foot forward." Bigger, from this perspective, is detrimental to African American progress.

Graham, who later became famous as the wife of W. E. B. Du Bois, commented privately to her future husband: "Last Sunday's *Times* carried a page on *Native Son*. That book turns my blood to vinegar and makes my heart weep for having borne two sons. They say it is a good book. Why?"[18]

The starting point for many reviewers was a place of denial. It was difficult for them to comprehend that the America they lived in could harbor a Bigger Thomas. Certainly they knew that there was inequality between Blacks and whites, but was it really that bad? Did American social conditions really drive Bigger—and others like him—to such states of hatred that they could kill in order to prevent acute psychological violation and constant emotional stress? Such responses simply meant that Wright had struck the chord he desperately wanted to strike: bringing to the attention of the masses of white Americans the realities of Black lives. Bigger might not have lived on their streets, but he lived in their cities. He might not have been with them in the movies they watched, but he was upstairs in the buzzard's roost drawing conclusions about how the lives of whites were depicted on screen in comparison to the life he lived every day. He might not have attended school with them, but he was aware—acutely so—of the limitations of education as they applied to him. And he might not have been hired into their factories, but he was well aware of the discrepancies in wages for any kind of job he might have been lucky enough to find, compared with the jobs young white men his age routinely claimed as theirs. Even as Bigger and his gang are hanging out on the streets, they must occasionally have seen young white men scurrying in their suits and ties to white-collar jobs that Bigger and his friends could only dream of having.

The mixture of reviews—complaint and compliment—perhaps measured the country's responses to African American males generally. Two hundred and fifty thousand copies of books sold would be a record at any period of American history, and it was certainly phenomenal in 1940. Still, the question remains—Why? Certainly there is no argument about Wright's skills as a writer, his ability to bring Bigger almost in living color to the eyes of his readers. However, there are additional reasons for the book's popularity. First, there is the blatant curiosity surrounding a text that deviated so dramatically from the previous norms in African American literature. Bigger is no Jimboy plucking the guitar as that character does in Hughes's *Not Without Laughter*. Nor is he a whoring Jake as in McKay's *Home to Harlem*, or the easy-going, party-hopping, entertaining Tea Cake of Hurston's *Their Eyes Were Watching God*. Bigger entered the literary world as an angry, transgressive young Black male with multiple chips on his shoulder and no viable outlets for his anger or his restlessness. No music could soothe his disappointments.[19] No religion could encourage him to trade this world for the next. And no sexual encounter with Bessie could provide more than temporary satiation, because his state of the blues is so profound that he cannot articulate it fully or point to an exterior source that would somehow make it better.

Second, voyeurism is a major factor in the novel's reception and popularity. *Native Son* enabled readers to gawk at Black American lives, from the limitations and restrictions in the opening rat scene, to the pleading and praying Mrs. Thomas on her knees before Mrs. Dalton, to the various dilapidated and overcrowded tenements that Bigger encounters on his run from the mob of policemen. There is also the voyeurism connected to Mary's death, decapitation, and burning as well as to Bessie's bludgeoning and the dumping of her body down the air shaft. With the Mary scene, it is almost comparable to witnessing King Kong in miniature (the original film premiered in 1933), with the Black male, always historically perceived as large and threatening, looming over the vulnerable white female and holding her fate in his hands.[20] With the Bessie scene, there is the horror and distancing from something perceived as monstrous, yet readers are unable to avert their eyes from it. How far will this monstrosity extend, some readers might have wondered. Then, to witness the "monster" be tamed, chained, and docile in court brings on another set of voyeuristic possibilities. Will he come from behind his shell and break down? Will the chains really hold him? Will he, despite being chained, try to escape? These questions might extend to wondering how many of the folks in the courtroom and surrounding the courthouse would eagerly accept an invitation to watch as Bigger is executed.

Perhaps the popularity of *Native Son*, third, was also a matter of the attraction that comes from being able to hold lightning in a bottle without the possibility of its striking one dead. Given how the general public responded to Robert Nixon, it would be foolish to assume that their responses to the fictional representation of a violent young Black man would all of a sudden have pivoted one hundred and eighty degrees. African American males were still fodder for imagining the violent and the damned. By creating Bigger, however, Wright has essentially domesticated the wild Black "beast," brought him home to capture and to justice by locking him "safely" into the pages of a book. He could now be caged and viewed (echoes of the Venus Hottentot) without the possibility of threat or danger. Wright thus ran a risk comparable to what Alice Walker did in publishing *The Color Purple* (1982), with its description of nearly monstrous Black male violence against Black women. By creating a Black male whom some readers could label monstrous, Wright handed over reins of judgment to those who could decide to be sympathetic or who could use his creation as fuel to start more fires of antagonism toward Black people. It is difficult to judge the impact of any literary creation upon social action and social responses to a given group, but it is perhaps not far-fetched to claim *some*—and reviewers such as Cohn and Rascoe would have spurred on such responses. Ultimately, Bigger is one example of lightning in a bottle, contained for a while but always with the potential to break out and strike without notice. That possibility ensured that Wright's creation would live on, no matter his detractors. Bigger would live on despite efforts to name him something

other than a twenty-year-old Black male whose hopes and aspirations are as American as those of any of the readers of *Native
Son,* no matter their claims to the contrary.[21]

Bigger ultimately urges readers to rethink issues of democracy
and citizenship, to move toward the cultural work that Wright
hoped his novel would achieve. By virtue of presenting his idle body
on the streets of Chicago or in the pool hall with his friends, Bigger brings home to sensitive readers the squandered potential highlighted in commercials for the United Negro College Fund—"A
mind is a terrible thing to waste." Just at the age when many young
people would be in the middle of a college career, Bigger is instead
plotting how to rob a store without being caught and sent back
to reform school. What, readers might wonder, has this young
man done to deserve such limited opportunities? What has influenced him to go down this particular path? How many times has
he sat and gawked at movies about white Americans that brought
home so vividly to him what was missing in his own life? At what
point could the trajectory of his life have been changed? What
would it have taken to bring about that change? (Certainly, the
ping-pong tables that Mr. Dalton has delivered to the South Side
Boys' Club are laughably insufficient.) And the questions could go
on. They are all ultimately as much about access to equal opportunity and the promises of democracy as they are about who is shut
in and who is shut out, who is native (entitled) and who is foreign
(outsider).

Bigger's mere presence upsets the comfort level of any reader
who believes in an America that should treat its citizens equally.
From the moment readers become aware that Bigger resides in a
single room with three other family members, to his violent crimes,
to his trek through Black tenements on the South Side of Chicago,
to his imprisonment and planned execution, they can only conclude—despite the horrible surface circumstances—that the key

LIGHTNING IN A BOTTLE

principles of democracy have failed in their unequal application to America's citizens. Business people, agents of law enforcement, newspaper reporters, attorneys, and all the folks who make up the masses inside and outside the courtroom where Bigger is put on display have set up walls to keep the Bigger Thomases outside what they consider "their" country. However, as Octavia E. Butler would make abundantly clear a half century later in *Parable of the Sower* (1993), the walls between those inside and those shunted to the outside will not hold. Life invades where figurative and literal walls would rather keep it out. Ambition, desire, and human longing will go where the powerful will not be able to hold them at bay. The sense of freedom that invades Bigger after actions that some observers might judge to be monstrous, warped, and perhaps even subhuman, cannot blot him from the literary landscape of American literature, the more specific landscape of African American literature, and the implicit claim to being a native American son that might be shocking but that cannot be denied. Thus Bigger prompted arguments, reactions, and controversies that still rage today. His claim upon readers' imaginations is no less potent in the twenty-first century than it was in the mid-twentieth century.

CHAPTER 4

———

Bigger from the 1950s to the Black Arts Movement

WITH *NATIVE SON,* Wright had become a literary sensation, and young writers throughout the world flocked to him. If the 1950s brought conflict with other Black writers over the idea of whether "protest literature" was possible or was literature at all, by the 1960s, with the rise of the Black Arts Movement, Wright's Bigger found a new and enthusiastic readership, and gained a new life: Bigger was indeed the precise person Black Arts writers and Black Power activists sought to reach. But first, he had to navigate the treacherous critical waters of the 1950s.

A decade after the publication of *Native Son* came the Korean War with its national disruption, and then came the stresses of the Cold War and budding McCarthyism. A young Black man in Chicago—not least, one with Communist sympathies—decrying the very basis on which the country was founded did not constitute a patriotic model. The need for American unity was matched in the critical realm when a prominent white scholar posited that

Native Son was less than representative of American creativity. In *Language as Gesture: Essays in Poetry,* R. P. Blackmur wrote in 1952: "*Native Son* is one of those books in which everything is undertaken with seriousness except the writing." He went on to maintain that the violence is "frivolous," called the class struggle a "fairy-tale," and concluded that "the book is a product of a sensibility so jaded by desperation that it could not reach the condition of imaginative honesty." The striking condescension in these comments is noteworthy for its implications of insiders and outsiders. Just as Bigger is outside the mainstream of American culture, so Blackmur considers Wright outside its creative traditions. This interloper might have published a novel, but he could not share unqualified artistic achievement in that effort. He may have been influenced by writers such as Henry James, Theodore Dreiser, H. L. Mencken, and John Dos Passos, but he could not claim artistic equality with them. Given the number of scholarly projects devoted to the artistry of Wright's novel, both at the time and in the future, Blackmur inadvertently insulted generations of scholars even as he insulted Wright.[1]

More than a decade after the publication of *Native Son,* a controversy developed surrounding Wright and Baldwin, which was echoed in yet another decade with critical exchanges between the literary critic Irving Howe and Ralph Ellison about a presumed controversy centering on Wright, Baldwin, and Ellison. These commentaries perhaps called more attention to Wright and Bigger than any other during the twenty-five years following the publication of *Native Son,* and are even more noteworthy because Ellison and Wright knew each other well (Ellison was best man at Wright's first wedding), and Wright served as a mentor to Baldwin. Yet both younger writers, in that tradition of offspring destroying their elders, felt it necessary to separate their writing philosophies and objectives from Wright's. Baldwin claimed that Wright was paranoid

about other writers stealing and also attacking his work, and Ellison articulated that Wright was one of his literary "relatives" but
not his literary "ancestor," the latter being a voluntary category
that enables any writer to select influences, as Ellison did with Ernest Hemingway, T. S. Eliot, and others. Wright had passed away
before Ellison's exchange with Howe, but he was around—though
living in France—when Baldwin published his essay.[2]

In "Everybody's Protest Novel," an essay by Baldwin published in the *Partisan Review* in 1949, surveying protest novels from
Uncle Tom's Cabin to *Native Son*, the comments on Wright take up
only a small and final portion of the piece. Baldwin began describ-
ing his disagreements with Wright about protest and literature,
which he developed in full a couple of years later. But these words
were the beginning of the end of Baldwin and Wright's relationship. Baldwin, almost twenty years Wright's junior, would have
been better served not to have mentioned Wright at all.

Baldwin developed his critique further in another essay for
the *Partisan Review*, "Many Thousands Gone" (October 1951). Here,
Baldwin asserted that it was "remarkable" that *Native Son* had
received the attention it did. Still, he objected primarily to what
he identified as the protest, naturalistic vein in which Wright wrote,
which, through Max's speech, dehumanized Bigger. "It is the question of Bigger's humanity which is at stake, the relationship in
which he stands to all other Americans—and, by implication, to
all people—and it is precisely this question which [Max's speech]
cannot clarify, which it cannot, in fact, come to any coherent
terms. He [Bigger] is the monster created by the American repub-
lic, the present awful sum of generations of oppression; but to say
that he is a monster is to fall into the trap of making him subhuman and he must, therefore, be made representative of a way of
life which is real and human in precise ratio to the degree to which
it seems to us monstrous and strange." Baldwin thus concluded

that Max's speech is "one of the most desperate performances in American fiction," an assessment that must surely have rankled Wright, since he had mentored Baldwin and been instrumental in his securing the prestigious Eugene F. Saxton Fellowship. Lack of loyalty was perhaps equally as painful as the terse dismissal of a substantial portion of the novel. Max's speech may fail from Baldwin's perspective, but it is a crucial act in Bigger's realizing that not all whites are a hateful, threatening blob. The speech enables Bigger to see through race to humanity and thus achieve one of the objectives for which Wright was writing.[3]

Still, Baldwin embraced the depiction of Bigger sufficiently to assert that "no American Negro exists who does not have his private Bigger Thomas living in the skull." Particularly troubling to Baldwin was the fact that Bigger was adrift in the world, apart from all sustaining African American cultural forms, including music and religion. By focusing exclusively on Bigger and his point of view, Baldwin claimed, "a necessary dimension has been cut away; this dimension being the relationship that Negroes bear to one another, that depth of involvement and unspoken recognition of shared experience which creates a way of life." Baldwin faults Wright for isolating Bigger. That accusation, however, warrants unpacking. Readers do see Bigger interacting with his gang in playful as well as serious and even dangerous moments. And they definitely get a sense of Mrs. Thomas's religious beliefs as well as those of the Black minister who comes to Bigger's cell. Certainly there is no scene of Mrs. Thomas in church or interacting with church sisters, and Bigger does not engage in a game of street ball with his friends, but to assert that there are no traditions among the Black characters is inaccurate.[4]

Following Wright's death, Baldwin reflected even more on their estranged relationship, which always centered on divergent views about the use of protest in literature. Wright consistently insisted, with Du Bois, that *all* literature contained protest, and Baldwin consistently begged to differ. From Baldwin's perspective, there was no way to save Bigger from monstrosity and dehumanization. Ironically, Baldwin later published *Another Country* (1962), a novel that a well-known critic labeled a work of "protest," which means that Baldwin reaped the same accusations that he had heaped on Wright's head.

It was the esteemed Jewish literary critic Irving Howe who granted Baldwin's novel its protest designation, in a 1963 essay in which he compared Wright, Baldwin, and Ellison, stirring the pot of controversy that led to a saucy brew of an exchange between Howe and Ellison. In the essay "Black Boys and Native Sons," Howe began by discussing the "painful rupture" between Wright and Baldwin. He then asserted that Baldwin and Ellison, natural descendants of Wright, can only move beyond "Wright's harsh naturalism" by recognizing that Wright was courageous enough to go first. Keep in mind that Howe was writing three years after Wright passed away. Also, Howe published the essay in his own magazine, *Dissent,* which means that there was no objective censoring of a white male, no matter how prominent or well-intentioned, referring to adult Black males as "Black boys" (even recognizing that Wright had titled his autobiography *Black Boy*). Howe used the phrase in the title and the final sentence of his essay. However, given the historical baggage that the word "boy" evokes in relation to Black men, a tone of hierarchical privilege overshadows the entire essay. (Howe also used "niggerboy"—without quotation marks—in what he hoped was a compliment to what Wright refused to become.) In addition, Howe lectured condescendingly when he noted what Baldwin "must" do in his role as a spokesperson for Black Americans. The crucial issue, however, is that, from Howe's perspective, Wright was the pioneer to whom both Baldwin and

Ellison owed a debt and whom they had betrayed by denying Wright's influence upon them. In an often-quoted passage, Howe asserted: "The day *Native Son* appeared, American culture was changed forever. No matter how much qualifying the book might later need, it made impossible a repetition of the old lies. In all its crudeness, melodrama and claustrophobia of vision, Richard Wright's novel brought out into the open, as no one ever had before, the hatred, fear and violence that have crippled and may yet destroy our culture."[5]

Howe recognized the value of Wright's inclination to protest and the validity of writing out of one's own experience; Baldwin agreed with writing out of one's experience but not to the extent that Wright does. Since both Baldwin and Ellison were trying to claim their artistic voices independent of Wright, Ellison was particularly annoyed with Howe claiming Wright as one of his direct predecessors. Howe's essay led to a back and forth with Ellison that went on for months. Mainly, Ellison declared that, although Wright was his friend, he "was no spiritual father of mine." He explained that he "rejected Bigger Thomas as any *final* image of Negro personality," but he nonetheless "recognized *Native Son* as an achievement; as one man's essay in defining the human condition as seen from a specific Negro perspective at a given time in a given place." Comparable to Dorothy Canfield Fisher's referring to *Native Son* as a "report," Ellison's use of the word "essay" similarly—and perhaps inadvertently—reduces the literary value of what Wright accomplished. Noteworthy as well is that there is no qualifier before "achievement." What kind of achievement? How significant? In defense of Howe accusing him of "filial betrayal," Ellison resorted to what appears to be jabs at Wright, whether he intended the phrasings that way or not. The candidness with which Ellison offered his comments and his constant challenges to Howe to continue the exchanges are also testaments to the fact that Wright was now deceased and thus unable to enter the conversation and offer something in his own behalf.[6]

What is significant about the months-long exchanges between Howe and Ellison, which are ostensibly about Wright, Baldwin, Ellison, reputation, and creative politics, is that they enabled a return to certain intellectual venues a concentration on Wright and *Native Son*. The numbers of publications on Wright had dropped sharply with his expatriation to France.[7] His death definitely revived some interest, but the Howe-Ellison exchanges brought *Native Son* and Bigger to the fore again. With the idea of protest being central and the implicit dehumanization that always seems to accompany that designation, it is worth pausing for a moment to reflect upon the idea of inhumanity and the impact it has—or not—in *Native Son*. Bigger may be comparable to a cornered rat in several portions of the novel, but he is *not* a rat, not the total "thing" that many characters in the text and many scholars and critics want to make him out to be. Lack of humanity has been referenced so much in discussions of the novel that it is used without examination, which constitutes a questionable position.

Despite his cruel and violent behavior, combined with his rejection of his mother's religion, Bigger does have a moral sense. He knows that robbing Blum's is wrong, just as he knew that stealing car tires was wrong, or certainly, at least, against the law (he ended up in reform school as a result). Bigger articulates aspirations and is otherwise capable of envisioning a different set of circumstances than the one in which he finds himself. Perhaps it is more fitting, therefore, to suggest that Bigger's human potential has been diminished acutely than to assert that he is devoid of humanity. Undoubtedly others in the text, such as Buckley and the newspaper reporters, attempt to reduce Bigger rhetorically to the subhuman, but readers and scholars might be better served not to follow that path.

The ties among protest, asserting humanity, and political activity were all central to the sixties. Those exchanges between Howe and Ellison were taking place against the backdrop of a budding Black Arts Movement, which would reach its peak in the late sixties. The militant young Black writers who defined that period were champions of social transformation and militant activism, the two-pronged approach to literary creation that thumbed its nose at Ellison's modernism of the 1950s. Bigger, who was certainly not an ideal for the integrationist mode of the 1950s, thus captured the imaginations of many of the Black writers in the sixties who believed that they should stride forward confidently, claim all social and legal rights available to them, and recognize no gap between what they portrayed and the lived experiences of Black people. Instead of the stagnant mirroring that might initially have defined Bigger, these writers felt that an activist mirroring was warranted; what they wrote was a formula for Blacks to take action and change their lives. Whether it was poets such as Nikki Giovanni and Sonia Sanchez urging Blacks to get the white out of their lives, or Haki Madhubuti inviting Blacks to embrace African traditions, or any number of young writers who called for reclamation and transformation, the sixties were a time when Black was declared beautiful, when old notions of "the Negro" gave way to new perceptions of "Blackness," "African Americans," and a turn toward Africa as an ancestral home. The revolutionary mood of the sixties made it possible for scholars and critics to reevaluate Bigger, to focus other lenses than "monstrous" and "pathological" upon him, and begin to see how his act of creation might be comparable to what many Black Nationalists felt was crucial in the sixties. The philosophy of Stokely Carmichael makes the point.

Articulator of Black Power, Carmichael, who later moved to Africa and took the name Kwame Ture, had no patience for gradualism or anything else that would slow down African American nationalist progress. The seeds of nationalism that Wright has written into Bigger's character thus resonated keenly with writers and activists of the sixties.

A key difference in Bigger's reception in the sixties versus earlier is the matter of audience. In 1940, Wright directed *Native Son* primarily to white readers whom he considered powerful enough to bring about changes in the social structure, and enhance educational and economic opportunities for Black people. If those readers truly sympathized with Bigger's plight, with the deprivations that had defined his life, with his exclusion from the promises of American democracy, then perhaps they might be inclined to do more than weep over his situation. Perhaps they might be inclined to take action to ensure that more young Black men received educational and job opportunities that would enhance their self-esteem and their ability to be valuable, contributing members of American society. On the other hand, the writers of the sixties had no such agenda. Why, Carmichael, echoing Lorraine Hansberry, asked, should Black people want to integrate into the burning house of America? Writers of the period echoed this sentiment by focusing their time and attention toward their own communities, toward the masses of Black people who, by transforming and loving themselves, redirecting their energies, and supporting their communities, could indeed achieve a level of sustainability and autonomy from white society that they had not previously enjoyed. As a disgruntled, deprived, and outcast American citizen, Bigger spoke directly to these writers. He was himself an embodiment of the kind of Black mind that these writers sought to reach with their revolutionary words.

Thus, while Wright himself might not have been a universally popular writer among a few of the firebrands of the sixties, Bigger had much to offer them.[8] As Russell Carl Brignano notes, prominent figures of the sixties such as Malcolm X, Stokely Carmichael, and LeRoi Jones (later known as Amiri Baraka) were cool toward Wright because they considered him "a white liberal's nigger." Margaret Walker also noted that Wright had a preference for white writers and thinkers, which implicitly questioned his Blackness. Over the course of their three-year friendship, during which they read and discussed numerous books (which Walker lists and comments upon in detail in her biography of Wright), read and revised each other's writing (beginning with early efforts in poetry), and generally worked to improve their creative abilities and output, Walker and Wright knew each other and each other's literary lives intimately. Walker observes that all of Wright's literary models were white and that white writers were the ones he most admired. She claims that "every positive force" in Wright's life "stemmed from white forces." She wonders "if it is malicious to think he would have been happier if he had been born white than he was as a black man." She contends further that she could not "think of a single black author during the thirties whom he admired to the point that he considered him the equal of any white writer. He had no great respect for the literary achievements of black people, not even Langston Hughes or W. E. B. Du Bois. Many black writers admired him, but when he picked his friends among writers they were all white." No matter Walker's entangled relationship with Wright, her observations of documentable facts give validity to her assessments.[9]

Given the uncompromising advocacy of Blackness that defined many of the young writers of the sixties, it is not surprising that some of them exhibited coolness to Wright's racial politics. After all, he was a willing bedfellow to white Communists and the white literary establishment generally. He lived in several homes and apartments of the Newtons (a prominent white female Communist and her Black husband), and he had not one but two white wives (a development about which Wright found himself on the defensive on many occasions). A superficial glance would suggest that Wright's Blackness could indeed be questioned, especially in a time when asserting one's Blackness was paramount in Black artistic circles. Wright might also have been considered an outsider to contemporary events in America, as he had abandoned his homeland for France in 1946. Bigger, on the other hand, was solidly American, solidly in the vein of Black struggle, solidly identifiable as a person of African descent whose opportunities had been limited severely by the laws and customs of American society. While some could have viewed Wright as a deserter, his character Bigger offered possibilities for transformation for America's Black people from fear of and mental consumption by whites to a healthier, more empowered lifestyle.

Bigger's life is ripe for the transformation that so many young Black writers of the sixties touted. Consider Nikki Giovanni's poem from 1968, "The True Import of Present Dialogue, Black vs. Negro (*For Peppe, Who Will Ultimately Judge Our Efforts*)." Here, Giovanni questions whether Black people have the ability to kill. Unquestionably they can die, Giovanni asserts, as she references the wars in which Black males have been sent to fight and have died, but . . . can they kill? She goes on to describe, among other violent acts, Blacks driving cars over "honkies" heads. Most important, she wonders, "Can you kill the nigger/ in you/ Can you make your nigger mind/ die Can you kill your nigger mind/ And free your black hands to/ strangle."[10]

Her questions might apply directly to Bigger. Throughout most of *Native Son,* Bigger is incapable of transforming himself from a scared Black male into something else, into someone who could claim at least a small portion of the best of himself. Implicit in

Giovanni's comments is that some Black folks in America have so internalized their second-class status that they cannot denude themselves of its influence, even when white people, who are directly responsible for Blacks having cultivated that sense of inferiority, are nowhere around. It is a mind thing, as Ellison's narrator declares at the end of *Invisible Man*; he has whipped everything except the mind. Patterns of behavior are so ingrained in Bigger, his mind so controlled by white-inflicted torment, that he cannot embrace the possibility of change, let alone participate in those changes, and therefore he is dumbfounded when Mary and Jan try to treat him as an equal. In his mind, Blacks will always be inferior to whites, and their physical relationships to whites will always be ones in which they are reduced to the less desirable space (for example, the back seat of any car that whites own instead of the front seat—unless he is there merely as chauffeur). Bigger is thus an excellent candidate for the transformation that Giovanni and others espoused during the sixties.

Similarly, Sonia Sanchez's position in "TCB," published in 1970, could easily apply to Bigger. Sanchez composes six stanzas of "wite/motha/fucka" (repeated three times in each stanza) followed by "whitey," "ofay," "devil," "pig," "cracker," and "honky" before she announces: "now. that it's all sed./ let's get to work." Recognizing the source of oppression is one thing. Naming that evil is another. Working collectively to eliminate that evil is something else altogether. From this perspective, Bigger is still in the name-calling stage. He can recognize and name the source of his oppression, but he has no viable means by which to move forward. Would he, for example, feel less oppressed if he had a job that would enable him to move his family out of their cramped kitchenette "apartment"? Does he have the presence of mind—or the desire—to go searching for such a job, and even if he did, could he land it? Does he have enough get-up-and-go about him to even care? Bigger has not yet put in the work necessary for the trans-formation to which Sanchez alludes, and he has no teacher like Sanchez to guide him. Indeed, Sanchez's entire career has been about articulating ways in which folks in Black communities can achieve healthy and happy lives. Bigger would be among those to whom Sanchez would address her advice for transformation as well as advice for activism, for she has poems in which she, like Giovanni, suggests that violence might be the best answer to al-leviating oppressive conditions.[11]

Sanchez and Giovanni, no matter the generational and life-style differences between them and Wright, nonetheless share with him the belief that words can be weapons. The Black Arts scholar Howard Rambsy describes the writers of the sixties trans-forming Wright's "words as weapons" concept (which Wright articulated after reading H. L. Mencken's essays), their poems becoming "'like little black spears,' to apply Henry Dumas's phras-ing, hurling militant critiques at barriers of injustice." For Wright's Bigger as well as this younger generation, the objective was the same: the surest way to garner the attention of a society unwilling to listen to polite requests or to grant lawfully submitted propos-als was to threaten or engage in violence.[12]

The violence that Bigger initially commits accidentally, then, is something that Black writers of the sixties wanted to occur de-liberately—even if that deliberateness might have been symbolic or metaphorical. Giovanni and Sanchez joined other writers of the period who shared similar sentiments. These writers—at least literarily—believed that violence was necessary to the healthy growth of Black human beings on United States soil, whether that violence needed to occur *within* the Black psyche or *against* the white oppressors of that psyche. Sadly, Bigger cannot execute their directive. The "nigger" in him, as Giovanni put it, is what Bigger is never able to kill.

However, the fact that he does commit violence aligns him with some of the characters who appear in fictional works of the sixties. Bigger's accidental murder of Mary and deliberate dispatching of Bessie connect him to the aggressive sentiments in Sam Greenlee's novel *The Spook Who Sat by the Door* (1969), which is about young Black men in Chicago who wage war against U.S.-owned facilities, including munitions works. Their leader is Freeman (symbolically named), a formally trained African American CIA operative who plots violent revolution against the United States. Freeman is the first African American CIA operative (referred to as "spooks"). During his training, he wears a mask of inconspicuousness even as he rises to the top of his recruitment class. His superb record ensures that the white higher-ups cannot deny him entry into the agency, where, for five years, he learns about weaponry, tactics, and covert operations. He leaves the CIA, goes to Chicago, and recruits as many Bigger Thomases as he can find to join him in attacking the United States. These disposable, throwaway young men, gang members like Bigger, are all unskilled but talented. Freeman gets them to trust him and leads them into cultivating their talents. He urges several young men to use their artistic gifts to draw recruitment posters. He persuades another young man to use his writing, poetic talent to become "propagandist" for the group. Yet another, a genius in mathematics, becomes the group's tactical expert.[13]

Freeman fills the gap between these Bigger Thomases and the Mr. Daltons of the world. Where the Daltons provide idle recreation (ping-pong tables for Chicago's South Side Boys' Club), Freeman provides young Black men purpose and solidarity. As mentor to the group, he offers support that no one has offered and enumerates expectations of which no one has ever considered these young men capable. Whereas the Bigger of *Native Son* could be viewed as a victim of circumstances in his killing Mary and intentional in his murdering Bessie, the Biggers that Freeman inspires learn from their mentor to cultivate intentionality in *all* their actions. They can name their disenchantment, as Sanchez points out, *and* they can elect to do something about it. They do not, as Bigger does, allow circumstances to happen to them.[14]

Having successfully completed several operations, Freeman and his recruits plan to spread the revolution from Chicago to other parts of the United States. Unfortunately, as with Wright's Bigger, there is a notable same-race casualty. Freeman, who has managed to remain under the radar at the CIA as well as in Chicago, finally becomes a suspect when an old girlfriend gets too observant. That leads to his Black policeman friend, Dawson, confronting Freeman and to Freeman killing Dawson. Freeman knows Dawson as well as Bigger knows Bessie, yet he concludes that Dawson must die for the revolution. While Bigger's action is certainly not imbued with the presumed nobility of Freeman's, the resulting death of a fellow Black human being is no less remarkable. Still, Greenlee achieves in fiction what Giovanni and Sanchez hint at and what Bigger vaguely envisions when he thinks that there ought to be someone who could bring the masses of Blacks together in a way that would be socially beneficial to and politically advantageous for them.

Thus, Bigger is at home among the writers of the sixties because of the fervent desire that they have for one thing: change. Like Wright, who wanted to change approaches to writing—from the acquiescent to the shocking—writers of the sixties wanted to move from traditional forms and create a "Black aesthetic," as Larry Neal commented in his essay "The Black Arts Movement."[15] Just as Wright felt that the aesthetic that African American writers who preceded him practiced was inadequate for what he hoped to achieve, so writers of the sixties believed that what they referred to as the "white" aesthetic, including the likes of William Faulkner, was no longer relevant for them. They wanted a Black aesthetic, just as Bigger wants a good job, a changed lifestyle, and a Black leader. They wanted to move away from Dick and Jane, the quintessentially representative white manifestation of Americanness, into a Black aesthetic, one that depended for its vibrancy upon African American cultural forms such as vernacular expressions and jazz music. The changes Wright and Bigger want might differ in degree from those of the writers and characters of the sixties, but they share the common recognition that America as currently constituted is not a place in which Black people can thrive.

Ultimately, Wright, Bigger, and the young people who followed them in the sixties wanted to change America from its exclusionary practices into something that would be viable for all American citizens, even if some of those citizens (Black people) had to formulate that something away from the eyes of prying whites. Politically, socially, personally, or however change gets written, it is the undergirding factor that leads to Bigger being very much a part of the social activist fervor of the sixties. Indeed, Bigger in this instance can be viewed as a big brother to the youngsters of the sixties who were just beginning to feel what he had felt so keenly from the moment he burst forth into the world in 1940.

CHAPTER 5

———

A Controversial Classic

THE DECADES following the sixties were crucial to the development of institutionalized study of African American literature. Several Black Studies programs had been formed in the sixties, and professors invited to teach in those programs were eager to populate their syllabi with African American writers, historians, sociologists, artists, and other professional producers of race-centered scholarship. Wright, *Native Son,* and Bigger all benefited from these developments. These years saw not only a consistent focus on Wright from scholars, but also a parallel development of more women scholars commenting on Wright's works. Whereas Dorothy Canfield Fisher might have been an exception as a woman writing about *Native Son* in 1940, by the 1970s literary criticism had moved from being primarily a male endeavor to one that included both genders. As more African Americans, male and female, received master's and doctoral degrees as a result of desegregation and admittance to some of the predominantly white graduate programs in literature, their visibility also enhanced the numbers of scholars and the range of treatments of African American literary works.

The institutionalization of African American literature took many forms: the production of bibliographies (frequently annotated and annual), bibliographic essays, indexes, biographical dictionaries, and encyclopedic entries. In this new canon, no writer was more prominent than Wright. Many collections of critical essays were published on his work, and his writing was collected in multiple anthologies. There were also special issues of several journals, as had been the case in the sixties, when *Negro Digest* devoted one such issue to Wright. Since African American literature as a distinct study in American universities was so new, numerous teaching guides appeared as well as personal accounts of teaching experiences in the classroom, including transracial accounts.[1]

The number of master's theses and dissertations completed on Black writers, of which Wright was the subject of an impressive share, was one of the most striking indications of how much African American literature was saturating American academia. Many of the writers of these projects cut their scholarly teeth by attending professional conferences such as the Modern Language Association (MLA) and the College Language Association (CLA), the latter being formed in 1937 by professors from predominantly Black colleges who were excluded from presenting at MLA. CLA went from being Eurocentric (as was the case with most historic Black colleges and universities before the mid-twentieth century) to having several sessions on African American writers each year at its annual convention. The critical atmosphere and the interest in African American literature were now very far removed from just a few decades earlier, when Wright had wondered if he could get *Native Son* published and had to agree to cuts to make it happen. It was becoming increasingly unimaginable that American literature, and especially African American literature, could exist without the centered inclusion of Wright.

Noteworthy as well in this period is the internationalization of scholarship on African American literature in the 1970s and 1980s. Wright's living in France obviously brought French attention to his work, and his writing was translated into more than a dozen languages, including French and German, allowing those scholars to access it in their own languages (Russian translations occurred before Wright left the United States). These decades also saw the beginning of Japanese scholars focusing on Wright, a pattern that continues into the twenty-first century.

Black studies and women's studies enjoyed parallel developments in American academia. What, then, were the implications of feminist literary criticism for *Native Son* and for Bigger in particular? Perhaps expectedly, the first Black women scholars focusing on *Native Son* approached the novel from traditional literary perspectives, such as the thematic and the formal. Maybe early African American female scholars did not want to attack a Black writer as prominent as Wright in a period when African American literary studies were in such an embryonic stage.[2] That changed slightly in 1982, when the novelist and poet Sherley Anne Williams published an article on Wright's treatment of Black female characters. Her comments align with general perceptions of Wright's attitudes toward Black women and move beyond that. Scholars who have written biographies of Wright and others who have published articles about him have commented on his troubled relationships with, if not downright hatred of, Black women. From the teenage Black girl he encountered in Memphis who wanted to marry him at first sight, to his denigration of the intellects of Black women he dated in New York, to his insistence to his white friend Jane Newton that Bessie *had* to die, Wright was ambivalent, sometimes hostile and denigrating, and never satisfied with or by Black women. His treatment of Bessie, therefore, deserves special scrutiny during this feminist era. Comments from a couple of scholars help to situate Wright's portrayal of Bessie and to make clear that she is indeed one of those characters whom Wright considered disposable.

In "Papa Dick and Sister-Woman: Reflections on Women in the Fiction of Richard Wright" (1982), Williams discussed Wright's problematic approach to his Black female characters. She asserted that "neither women characters nor 'women's questions' figure centrally in Wright's fiction; when they appear at all, they are subsumed under larger political or philosophical themes." Wright's treatment of Black female characters positioned him as both "sexist and racist," Williams argued; "Wright seldom loved his black female characters and never liked them, nor could he imagine a constructive role for them in the black man's struggle for freedom." His attitudes, she continued, provide justification for "the hunger of his black heroes for that forbidden American fruit, the white woman, and the validity of his own use of the white woman as the ultimate symbol of the black man's freedom."[3]

Williams nonetheless recognized, and rightly so, that anything she offered about Wright and *Native Son* would ultimately be to the good of Wright, as he was being centered in the American literary canon: "This discussion of an important subtext in Wright's work can even be seen as casting a deeper and truer light over his reputation, rather than diminishing it, for his place in the tradition does not depend upon these often scandalous portraits of black women." Even though Williams considered Wright "the father of modern Afro-American literature," she questioned whether he perhaps ultimately executed a disservice to the literature. "Wright also fathered a bastard line, racist misogyny—the denigration of black women as justification for glorifying the symbolic white woman—and male narcissism—the assumption that racism is a crime against the black man's sexual expression rather than an economic, political, and psychological crime against black people—that was to flower in the fiction of black writers in the late sixties and early seventies."[4]

African American writers and scholars who dared to question the male-dominated enterprise of creating works about Black lives often found themselves the butt of criticism. Calvin Hernton later argued about this period in an often-cited essay, "The Sexual Mountain and Black Women Writers" (1984), that Wright's treatment of Black women was in direct contrast to the rise of Black feminist writing of the 1970s and 1980s. "In *Native Son*," Hernton wrote, "Richard Wright portrays Bigger Thomas's mother and sister 'realistically' as decrepit, nagging bitches; Bessie Mears, Bigger's girlfriend, is a pathetic nothing." Near the end of the twentieth century, Arnold Rampersad echoed Williams as well: "Many feminists understandably found the body of [Wright's] work less than appealing; Wright's fiction offers few examples of women, especially black women, who might be admired for intelligence or strength of character. Indeed, in his fiction he sometimes seems to fear and dislike black women." The environment that Williams, Hernton, and Rampersad reference helps to explain the fluctuating reactions to *Native Son* during the sixties and following.[5]

Wright's portrayal of Bessie is certainly one of the scandalous portraits Williams cites, and Bessie definitely falls short of the white Mary in just about every category imaginable.[6] The damning evidence against Wright is that he portrays a Black female character in ways that allow the romantic interest in her life to abuse her consistently and get away with it, until he finally puts her in a position that, from his perspective, warrants his killing her. Wright suggests thereby that Bessie is as expendable, as disposable to Bigger as the larger society deems Bigger is to it. The power Bigger wields over Bessie is comparable to the power whites wield over him that makes him feel so helpless in their presence. Wright uses Bessie to shed light on Bigger's character and what he wants readers to understand about Bigger's position rather than show-casing any intrinsic value she has. Bessie, one of the hard-working masses of Blacks in urban areas in the first half of the twentieth century, reflects the drudgery that characterized so many migrants from the South who believed that moving north would make their lives better, only to discover that the conditions under which they were forced to live short-circuited all those expectations.

Just as Wright drew his portrait of Bigger from real life per-sonalities, he also mirrored life with Bessie's violent relationship with Bigger. Sociological studies reveal that domestic violence was generally accepted during the 1930s and 1940s.[7] Contemplation of the ever-presence of such violence in the twenty-first century makes it easy to imagine its prevalence in the first four decades of the twentieth century. Wright, then, captures a feature of the society to which both Bessie and Bigger are heir. In the absence of any sense of worth in the larger white world and intuiting his lack of value generally, Bigger, in classic pattern, turns his aggres-sive tendencies toward those close to him, namely his family, his fellow gang members, and Bessie. Such a recognition in no way condones domestic violence; rather, it is to note that Bessie and Bigger find themselves against a backdrop of societal abuse that occurs across all racial groups and all socioeconomic groups. Big-ger wields power over Bessie as the society wields power over him. The transformed Bigger that readers see in his interactions with Black characters (transformed from his cowering in the presence of whites) is a symptom of a disease that strikes all society but that affects him more because the parameters in which he oper-ates are so limited.

Bigger takes advantage of Bessie sexually, emotionally, and physically. As Sondra Guttman commented in 2001: "Wright reveals that sexual violence within the black community is, in part, a prod-uct of the political anger provoked by the disjunction between the expectations that prompted so many blacks to leave the rural south and the exploitation they experienced when they arrived. This disappointment is displaced onto the black woman's body insofar as her body serves as the symbolic site of the rural idyll. Wright is careful to show, however, that this association between the black female body and the pre-urban south exists in the mind of the black man."[8] Bigger is guilty of threatening and slapping Bessie, of using brute force against her when she is initially reluc-tant to join his kidnap plan, and finally murdering her because he believes she is too weak to accompany him and will reveal his guilt to authorities if he leaves her behind. A brief interaction between the two characters serves to show domination and submission, physical and emotional abuse. Bessie is distraught, crying, and on the verge of collapse as she sits against the wall of the tene-ment to which Bigger has taken her to show her where she needs to be to receive the ransom money. When he admonishes her to do better, she replies:

> "I'd rather have you kill me now," she sobbed.
>
> "Don't you say that again!"
>
> She was silent. His black open palm swept upward in a swift narrow arc and smacked solidly against her face . . .
>
> "Bigger. . . . "
>
> "Come on, now."
>
> "Take me home."
>
> "You going to do it?"
>
> She did not answer.
>
> "You already in it," he said. "You got part of the money."
>
> "I reckon it don't make no difference," she sighed.

"It'll be easy."

"It won't. I'll get caught. But it don't make no difference. I'm lost anyhow. I was lost when I took up with you. I'm lost and it don't matter. . . ."[9]

Faced with Bigger's insistency and his brute force, Bessie is indeed lost. She has no one to turn to, and there is no one who can rescue her from her bad choices. She is caught in Bigger's domestic abuse as surely as the policemen will catch Bigger. To Bigger, Bessie becomes merely another set of hands, another set of eyes, another set of feet to move into position to receive the money that he hopes to extract from the Daltons.

Bessie is thus a commodity to Bigger, a body, comparable to the ways in which Black bodies generally serve a use value to the larger society in terms of muscle they provide to perform the dirty and menial jobs that keep the country operational. Bessie's value is similarly in direct proportion to Bessie's usefulness. When Bigger needs/wants sex, he goes to Bessie. When he is stressed after he has killed Mary, he goes to Bessie. When he needs an accomplice in trying to carry out his flimsy kidnap plan, he goes to Bessie. Outside of his family and his gang, whom he would never trust with what he has done, Bessie is the only character to whom he can go. Yet, as his brother Buddy makes clear, Bessie can be traded out for another girlfriend at a moment's notice, which means that Buddy and Bigger share a system of values about Black women and their roles. Again, expendability is crucial to how they think. Thus, there is nothing about Bessie that keeps Bigger attached to her other than the fact that she fits the requirement for female companionship. Expediency and expendability coexist in evaluations of Black female worth to the Thomas brothers and, as will become increasingly clear, especially to Bigger.

Although Bigger is not on trial for having raped Bessie, he does indeed rape her. What he may have wanted to do with Mary, he actually does to Bessie. In a freezing, funky, abandoned tenement, and against her protests, Bigger concentrates on his sexual desires and ignores completely Bessie's admonitions to him, no matter their soft-spokenness, to desist. From "Please, Bigger," to "Bigger. . . . *Don't*," to "her fingers spreading protestingly open, pushing him away," to "*don't Bigger don't*," he makes Bessie suffer what he has not done with Mary. Again, Bessie is simply a body, a vessel for the depositing of the sperm that Bigger so desperately feels he must deposit in order to relieve his tension. While he admits that he figuratively rapes when he thinks about white people, he never acknowledges that he rapes Bessie. In the devaluing of Black women that undergirds the text, Bessie suffers and dies because Bigger cannot see and acknowledge the very humanity in her that he so wishes the larger world would see in him.[10]

In her discussion of the female characters in *Native Son,* Carol Henderson observes that "Wright's bold literary depiction of the vile dismemberment of one Mary Dalton and of the doubly brutal rape and murder of one Bessie Mears ushers in a new era of literary violence against women that borders on the sadistic" and also served as the impetus for a couple of African American women writers, namely Gwendolyn Brooks and Ann Petry, to compose works that overwrite or revise what Wright did with Black women on his urban landscape. In both Petry's and Brooks's works, Black women figure as central, complex heroines in an urban environment shaped by racism, poverty, and misogyny. In Petry's *The Street* (1946), protagonist Lutie Johnson fights mightily against forces that could destroy her and her family. She works as a domestic in Connecticut, auditions for singing gigs when she returns to New York, and studies in the evenings to become a legal secretary. Though she loses in the end, her desire to succeed far exceeds anything Bigger ever attempts. Brooks's Maud Martha, the titular character in this 1953 narrative set in Chicago, must fight interracial as well as intra-racial prejudice. Her dark skin makes her less desirable, and she is never quite sure that she retains her husband's affection. Yet she perseveres despite the odds and remains stable and vibrant at the end of the novel.[11]

In the pattern of call and response so crucial to African American culture, therefore, Petry and Brooks "respond" to Wright's "misogynistic call" as they salvage characters and spaces that Wright has denigrated. Henderson's is one of several articles in the past few decades focusing on expansive and sensitive interpretations of Wright's treatment of women, especially Black women, in *Native Son*. The increase in the numbers of such publications is again a testament to *Native Son*'s journey to the center of American and especially African American literary studies.[12]

More recently, the scholars Kimberly Drake and Andrew Warnes have published essays offering feminist perspectives on *Native Son*. Drake shares my position that "rape" refers to much more than the penetration of a body and can reference a history of psychological violation or suggest instances in which Black subjects are denuded of voice and action; however, Drake completes a much more extensive analysis than I attempt. Unquestionably, Bigger rapes Bessie. He also asserts that he symbolically rapes Mary and indeed the entire society that makes him feel so useless and insignificant. Bigger is in turn "raped" by that society. In traditional sexual terms, he is forced to be passive in his own violation. He is raped physically and psychologically by a society that erases his essence and considers his body a mere cipher on which it can write whatever it wishes. Arguably, Bigger is essentially a zombie performing at the will of the folks who have saturated his mind and who control his body. Bigger is owned/possessed just as he owns/possesses Bessie's body. As Drake, referencing Marlon Ross, observes: "'rape' signifies not only 'men's domination over women,' but a less gender-specific domination of African Americans through 'sexualized violence from the period of slavery forward.'" Drake continues: "Rape, then, covers not only actual physical penetration but also the emasculating penetration of the white gaze that carries with it the threat of (sexualized) violence. Indeed, Bigger experiences the feeling of being penetrated and 'contaminated' by Mary and Jan at various moments during the evening."[13]

Thus Bigger and Bessie are positioned similarly, though Bigger believes he is superior to Bessie. From his perspective, Bessie does not think or analyze. She is blind to the social conditions of her existence. She is a drunk for whom alcohol serves as her religion. Yet, for all his supposed insight, Bigger is ultimately just as vulnerable as is Bessie. His budding awareness of the socioeconomic conditions of Blacks does not separate him from the masses of those Blacks. He is still viewed as the oversexed monster, the beast who would destroy white womanhood. Drake's detailed analysis of the relationship makes clear the continuing evolution of scholarly treatment of the feminist issues in the text, especially when those issues can reasonably reach beyond gender into new levels of interpretation.

So too with Andrew Warnes's "Fatal Eyeballing: Sex, Violence, and Intimate Voyeurism in Richard Wright's *Native Son*" (2017). Warnes explores in depth the influences of Poe, Dostoevsky, and Henry James upon Wright in the way that he treats Mary's death. In place of historical "reckless eyeballing," in which Black males, in the manner of Emmett Till, were murdered for looking at white women, Warnes uses motifs from crime fiction and movies to illustrate how viewing women unobtrusively contributes to the "intimate voyeurism" that characterizes several of the works he considers. Warnes suggests that what happens between Bigger and Mary in Mary's bedroom "looks ahead to 1970s feminism's incipient concern with the erotic exploitation of women's bodies." This would ultimately be theorized as the concept of *scopophilia*. Bigger looks in the rearview mirror at Mary while she and Jan are making out, and he looks at her perfectly composed corpse once he has killed her. His actions fit, Warnes argues, with those of several other central characters in movies, stories, and novels. Such an analysis suggests the extent to which Wright criticism connects with other arenas of critical inquiry, in this case crime fiction and film studies, and illustrates that, even when those arenas overlap with the racial issues, Wright's complex work moves beyond any attempt at confining critical interpretations. Warnes thus joins Drake and many other scholars in illustrating that Wright criticism is alive and well in the twenty-first century and that there are still unexplored horizons of commentary to which it can aspire.[14]

Prominent writers, scholars, critics, and cultural observers across several decades have confirmed the place that *Native Son* and Bigger hold in American literary culture. Eldridge Cleaver, who vigorously defended Wright against Baldwin's accusations about protest fiction, asserted in *Soul on Ice* (1968): "Of all Black American novelists, and indeed of all American novelists of any hue, Richard Wright reigns supreme for his profound political, economic, and social reference." Maryemma Graham, in a special issue of *Callaloo* devoted to Wright in 1986, maintained that the questions and debates he occasions are "sufficient justification for claiming his continued literary and intellectual importance." In 1993, Henry Louis Gates, Jr., wrote, "if one had to identify the single most influential shaping force in modern Black literary history, one would probably have to point to Wright and the publication of *Native*

Son, his first and most successful novel." In 1995, Arnold Ramp-ersad declared that Wright's work "moves into the twenty-first century on solid ground" and that, among African American writ-ers, Wright is "perceived" "as one of the landmark authors in the two-hundred-year history of the literature."[15]

Whatever scholars may conclude about Bessie, Bigger, Mary, or any other character in *Native Son,* their impressions, either positive or negative, ultimately serve in the process of installing the novel in the canon of American literature. By whatever stan-dard of measure one applies—books and articles published, dis-sertations written, conference presentations made, speeches delivered, or bibliographies compiled—*Native Son* has become a classic in American and world literature. It has also crossed dis-ciplines and informed such intellectual fields as law. There may have been periods when less attention was focused on the text, but it has *always* received attention. In his second annotated bib-liography on Wright, Kinnamon included 8,660 items that men-tion Wright or his work that were published between 1983, when his first annotated bibliography left off, and 2003. He also included an addenda of 1,295 works published between 1934 and 1982.[16]

International focus on Wright continues to be as constant as it is nationally; indeed, scholars from around the globe have fre-quently come to the United States for conference presentations on Wright as well as for special conferences about him. One such conference, for example, was held at the University of Iowa as early as 1971. In November 1985, at an International Symposium held at the University of Mississippi in Oxford, numerous international scholars appeared on the program. The summer 1986 issue of *Cal-laloo,* which Graham edited, is a special edition of selected papers from that symposium. In the fall of 1989, the *Mississippi Quarterly* published the Richard Wright issue, to which Keneth Kinnamon contributed an annotated bibliography of items on Wright that appeared between 1983 and 1988. An international symposium was held at the Gorky Institute of World Literature in Moscow in July 1989. In 1990, Harold Bloom edited *Bigger Thomas* in the Chelsea House "Major Literary Characters" series. *Obsidian* devoted a special issue to Wright in 2010.[17]

According to Kimberly Drake, "The various Richard Wright Centennial conferences that occurred all around the world in 2008 are testaments to the staying power of his body of work to the present day." There were also conferences in Wright's homespace of Natchez, Mississippi, as well as in Salt Lake City.[18]

Publisher investment is one of the surest indications that a writer is ensconced on the American literary landscape, and *The Richard Wright Encyclopedia* was published in 2008. That investment was made even clearer when the Library of America published several of Wright's works. *Native Son* was institutionalized enough for the Modern Language Association, the premier professional organization for literature and language teachers in the United States, to devote one of its "Approaches to Teaching" volumes to the novel, which also speaks to its cultural centering in the American literary imagination (*Approaches to Teaching Wright's Native Son*, 1997). This was matched with the founding of the Richard Wright Society, a constituent organization of the American Literature Association, which is in turn a subsidiary of the Modern Language Association. In 2011, *Native Son* was one of the novels treated on the "Re-Reading Classic Works in Literature" panel at the South Atlantic Modern Language Association (SAMLA) convention held in Atlanta. Of note as well is that, during the 2014–2015 academic year, a doctoral student at the University of Alabama took *Native Son* from the hallowed halls of academia to inside the walls of a maximum security prison where she taught a course in African American literature. Then, to cap off these signals of institutionalization, Cambridge University Press published *The Cambridge Companion to Richard Wright* in 2019.[19]

All of these adventures and events point to how Wright and *Native Son* have become integral parts of American and international literary and cultural exchanges. Today, Bigger is built into the very DNA of American literature.

CHAPTER 6

Bigger on Bigger

BIGGER MOVES through *Native Son* at the mercy of a narrator who offers up his interior life. Readers are locked into his consciousness and travel along with him, but what he has to say for and about himself pales in comparison to the thousands upon tens of thousands of words that the narrator offers about him. What if we consider, then, only what Bigger says in the most unfiltered moments in the novel? What do those comments reveal about Bigger and the themes that Wright wants to develop? Following, I offer a selection of some of Bigger's words and my responses to them.

> "I could fly one of them things if I had a chance. . . . I *could* fly a plane if I had a chance."

Deprivation is the essence of Bigger's complaint—what the larger, white society keeps from him. His complaint echoes Wright's epigraph from Job: "*Even today is my complaint rebellious, My stroke is heavier than my groaning.*"[1]

Two questions arise. First, why would Wright, an avowed

Communist and rejecter of Black folk religion, undergird his text with a *Christian* epigraph?[2] Second, where is there evidence that Bigger has tried to alleviate his suffering—that is, what responsibility does an individual have to attempt to improve his or her lot despite the odds? Having dropped out of school in the eighth grade, Bigger has intellectual abilities that fall far short of admission to flight school, which means that there is a great gap between the reality of his existence and expression of that reality. Braggadocio leads Bigger to claim what is a long way from where he lives and breathes. The reiterative expression will occur again and gives the impression that Bigger believes he can speak the intangible into being. His lack of preparation gets subsumed under his stronger desire to complain about the society, to whine about his position in it, which is one of stasis for which he can see no outlet.

Underlying Bigger's words is also an implicit, though nascent, understanding of the way American democracy operates. Others (mostly whites, though this is the era of the Tuskegee airmen, about whom Bigger has probably never heard) *can* fly planes, but Bigger perceives himself as denied that possibility. He inherently understands who can claim the privileges of American citizenship and who cannot. Bigger is outside looking in, as he will later express so poignantly. His is therefore a repetitive cry of longing, a complaint against restriction and limitations. If "they" (those ubiquitous, powerful, mostly unseen white controllers of destiny) will not allow him to fly planes, then perhaps that will be possible in the new world order that Wright envisions if oppressed Blacks and whites everywhere join together in a fight against capitalism. The theme of a nationalism that opposes Communism and that works to negate naturalism is thus inherent in Bigger's comment.[3]

"Let's play 'white'."[4]

This is thoroughly age *in*appropriate activity for Bigger and Gus (Gus's hesitation also signals discomfort). Playing such a game—with a different subject focus—is expected of elementary school children when they become "teacher" or "doctor" or "mommy and daddy," not what twenty-year-old Black males, so-called toughs, on the streets of Chicago might perform. Gus's reluctance is understandable (he looks "wearily" at Bigger), but he is finally drawn in because of Bigger's insistence. The sketch reveals the extent to which Bigger and those around him have been saturated with the kind of American capitalist practices and white American ideals Toni Morrison presents in *The Bluest Eye*. There is no escape from whiteness and what it represents, not even in one's mind. A consideration of Bigger's and Gus's reactions in the movie theater reinforces this idea. Everything they witness highlights the contrast between whites and Blacks, between haves and have-nots, between the power brokers and the powerless.

The exchange raises another issue: role modeling. If the only models for successful behavior on United States soil belong to whites, then how can non-whites ever expect to achieve anything and be successful? Bigger and his companions are perpetually outside—outside of job possibilities, outside of desirable living spaces, outside of educational opportunities. They may imitate whites as much as they wish, but they can never transform themselves, à la the characters in George Schuyler's *Black No More* (1931), into white human beings. Playing white brings home to Bigger repeatedly that he is dismissed, devalued, alien, and expendable in the society he calls home.

"Every time I think about it I feel like somebody's poking a red-hot iron down my throat. Goddammit, look! We live here and they live there. We black and they white. They got things and we ain't. They

do things and we can't. It's just like living in jail. Half the time I feel
like I'm on the outside of the world peeping in through a knot-hole
in the fence. . . ."[5]

Here, in contrast to the sketch about playing white, Bigger
addresses directly the negative internalization of devaluing that
controls his life. His mind is alive and active every day, torment-
ing him in every circumstance in which Bigger finds himself. The
visceral, emotional reaction to racial oppression is matched with
an awareness of separation and the constant enforcement of outsider status. Central to Bigger's frustration is economics. He and
his family are *always* in need of money, but he has no viable option
for ensuring a steady income. He can therefore not fulfill the American Dream or even the mundane expectation that a man should
be able to support his family. His frustration here, though, is more
for himself than his family. Resources that would enable him to
live comfortably are located elsewhere in the city, and that elsewhere marks the distinction between "Black" spaces and "white"
spaces, Black lack and the possibility of white largesse to fill those
lacks. In a few words, including the striking poetic image of "a
knot-hole in the fence," Bigger illustrates his awareness of outsider
status and registers his frustration that the situation will probably
not change any time soon.

Bigger's cursing reaction contains the anger that he feels and
that will grow as the text progresses. Significantly, he can express
his anger and frustration only in the safe environment of sharing
with Gus. Together, away from the eyes of family or whites, they
can unmask with each other and rail against their social and economic circumstances. Keep in mind, though, that this comment appears after Bigger learns about the Dalton job. He is railing against
the status quo, but he has not yet exerted the energy to get the
job. So, his complaint has to be set against the unconvincing way

in which he evinces true interest in the job possibility. Indeed, arguably, it is only after seeing Mary on the screen in the theater that he decides—finally—that he will go to the Dalton home. Readers must place Bigger's complaints, then, against what he actually does—or does not do—in trying to improve his position. It is easy to complain, but how many times has he actually gone out looking for work? Recall that conversation with his family in which Mrs. Thomas and Vera castigate Bigger for his unwilling-ness to do better. How much time, then, does he spend simply loafing around the pool hall or hanging out in the movies instead of pounding the pavement looking for work? Wright has primed readers to see the web of naturalistic circumstances in which Big-ger is caught, but they can also see the small places in which there are tears in that net, tears that might have allowed brief if not permanent escapes.

"I—I. . . . I don't want to go in. . . ."[6]

This passage, in which Bigger expresses his reluctance to go into Ernie's Kitchen Shack with Mary and Jan, captures in a very short exchange the history of interaction between Blacks and whites, and it contrasts sharply with his earlier aggressiveness in talking with Gus and with the violence he displays in the pool hall. The passage highlights the sense of place that I discussed earlier. As a Black male driving whites, Bigger believes (and society has taught him) that it is not his place to share meals at the same table with whites. Just as Mary and Jan have made him tremendously uncom-fortable by forcing him to ride in the front seat with them, their requesting that he join them in Ernie's is equally so. The hesitation ("I—I") shows that Bigger knows the history well, even if Mary and Jan are trying to subvert it. His stuttering could also mean that he is aware that, by saying no, he is essentially going against an order that a white person has given him. The fact that he *dares* to say no—even hesitantly—foreshadows some of the feelings he will express about such transracial interactions later on.

Here is one of the few instances when Bigger actually expresses a desire to a white person. Mostly he is acquiescent with his "Yes, sir" and "Yes, ma'am" responses. Perhaps this sentence shows a glimmer of the Bigger who can indeed rebel, the Bigger who is capable of taking the lives of two people. In this tiny window of no-ness, of saying what he wants or prefers, Bigger gives readers a glimpse of the inner life that all the whites around him refuse to recognize and accept. Instead of being the cipher into which Mary and Jan can simply pour their requests, Bigger resists. It does not matter that he ultimately gives in and goes into Ernie's. What is important here is the glimpse of resistance, the expression of a want to a white person, something that Bigger is usually unable to do.

"I'll fix it, mam." "I'll fix it." "I'll fix it, mam."[7]

These sentences, which occur after Bigger has smothered Mary, then decapitated and burned her body, are in response to Peggy's requesting that Bigger add more coal to the furnace. Knowing what he has put inside the furnace the night before, Bigger speaks action without performing action. His feet do not move toward the furnace. Instead, he attempts to assure Peggy that he will do what is requested. Simultaneously, he attempts to reassure himself—as he will on several occasions about different actions—that he is in control. These responses are early indications that Bigger is absolutely *not* in control, that he cannot "fix" the situation with the furnace, with having killed Mary, or, later, with the kidnap note or with forcing Bessie to flee with him. These sentences are the beginning of events unraveling completely and of

Bigger being pushed farther and farther away from "fixing" any part of the killing/kidnapping/fleeing situation.

As with the repeated assertion that he could fly a plane if given a chance, Bigger seems to suggest that, if he speaks something aloud, then it will gain more credibility, that it might move toward realization. Just as he has no credentials to fly a plane, however, he has no requisite skills to conceal a killing or to carry out his hastily drawn up kidnap plan. The individual he directs his "fix it" sentences to, Peggy, is a member of the continuing white audience to whom he plays his ill-hatched plan. He will be no more success-ful with them in the events surrounding Mary's death than he has been with any other interaction with whites in the novel. If he cannot distract Peggy, who is a servant and at the lowest level of white hierarchy, from focusing on the furnace, then he will have no chance of fooling Britten and the reporters who are much more adept at examining crime scenes and uncovering evidence than Bigger could ever imagine being.

> "You scared? You scared after letting me take that silver from Mrs. Heard's home? After letting me get Mrs. Macy's radio? You scared now?"[8]

An exchange between Bigger and Bessie after Mary's death, this passage is revealing for alerting readers to Bigger's previous criminal trespasses and the part Bessie played in them. They have employed a scheme that was common in the early twentieth cen-tury. A Black maid working in an exclusive white home would allow her boyfriend or other Black male friends access to the space, from which they would selectively steal valuable items and sell them (even Malcolm X documented such schemes in his autobiography). What Bessie has enabled Bigger to do is further evidence that he is not a completely innocent victim of ghetto life. He has made choices that led, initially, to committing crimes that did not result in bodily harm. His previous actions also close the moral gap between intentionality and unintentionality in Mary's death; if Bigger stands on the edge of morality with things, then why not with human life? The tendency to lawlessness thus informs what Bigger plans to do with the kidnapping scheme after Mary's death. That death might have been an accident, but Bigger is willing to capitalize on it by embracing his previous and ongoing criminal tendencies.

The passage also serves as a prelude to Bigger's manipulation of Bessie. Dangling the money from Mary's purse before her, he plays upon her financial insecurity as well as her love for him. He also echoes the charge that Gus has leveled against him earlier—that he is afraid to rob Blum's because the owner is white. Taunting Bessie with the charge of fear will either force her to overcome it or lead her to embrace it, which means she would be diminished in her own as well as Bigger's eyes. Taunting Bessie allows Bigger to alleviate some of his own tension, for he is indeed afraid. Loud-voiced braggadocio or insult to those around him (as in the case when discussing robbing Blum's) allows Bigger to try to calm his own nerves. Also, in showing Bessie's complicity in Bigger's robbing of white homes, Wright lets readers see that the social circumstances that lead ghetto dwellers to commit crimes are not restricted by gender.

> "Well, nothing, suh. Miss Dalton told me to take the trunk down so I could take it to the station this morning; and I did."[9]

James Baldwin was one of the critics who accused Wright of not evoking African American folk practices, indeed of abandoning African American folk culture. This comment from Bigger (which he addresses to Mr. Dalton), and several others that follow, are instances in which Bigger is mask-wearing, which is one of the operational modes of the trickster and one of the cardinal features of African American folk tradition. Bigger dons the mask to play the Daltons about Mary's directives to him. If he can convince them that he has followed Mary's instructions explicitly, then he may be able to direct suspicion away from himself. Amorality and misdirection are key components of mask-wearing, so Bigger has no qualms about lying or implicating Jan. During this scene, therefore, Bigger tries hard to appear as the compliant servant, the faithful and dutiful "nigger," the ignorant Black man who could not possibly have the brain power to do anything against powerful whites. Even as he wears the mask, though, he is taking pleasure in the fact that he is indeed using his brain to fool powerful whites, to play to their stereotypes about Blacks and thus remain one step ahead of them in whatever they do to uncover Mary's whereabouts.

Bigger's mask-wearing continues throughout the early parts of the "Flight" section of the novel. He initially misdirects questions from Britten as well as from the reporters. Through body language and speech, he is mostly successful in deflecting attention from himself. To these men, he presents as a stupid darky who is too ignorant to know that he should remove ashes from the furnace. Later, after he is caught, his interrogators are initially unwilling to believe that he is smart enough not only to have killed Mary but to have planned a kidnap scheme. His eventual capture does not erase the effectiveness with which he initially adopts a mode of operation that too many critics have accused Wright of abandoning.

"Leave me alone." "Leave me alone! Leave me alone!"[10]

Still in the "Flight" section, Bigger encounters Jan after he has falsely accused Jan of having a hand in Mary's disappearance. He speaks these words to Jan after Jan requests an explanation. The sentences indicate the unraveling of the coolness that Bigger exhibited when he wore the mask and interacted with Mr. Dalton, the detectives, and the reporters. Here, he is reverting quickly to a scared Black "boy" and devolving into the dismantled state of being that will lead to his capture. Initially, with the screaming imperative, Bigger shows that whatever hesitation he had to speak up to whites has disappeared. In addition, he pulls a gun and comes close to shooting Jan. The repeating of the order to Jan and the screaming exclamation points indicate that Bigger is fast losing control of his emotional state just as he has lost control—if he ever had any—of the situation at the Dalton home.

This break between Bigger and Jan, the white Communist, also suggests that a pathway forward that unites Black and white workers of the world may not be the most effective way of addressing the situation of Black Americans. For all his good intentions, Jan, like Max, does not really *see* Bigger. Jan has failed to take into consideration the imposition that he and Mary have made upon Bigger earlier. If the so-called futuristic union of Blacks and whites is to go only in one direction—white toward Black—then how can there be true unity and cooperation? Jan, like Mary, is guilty of cultural voyeurism and, indeed, a level of racial condescension. Certainly folks across cultures and races need to get to know each other, but there is a baseline level of interaction that both Jan and Mary have skipped. They want instant results instead of realizing that *true* transracial understanding takes extended time, repeated encounters, and mutual cooperation. It cannot be accomplished on a single evening with a trip to a restaurant and with the good-hearted white liberal passing along his political pamphlets to the uninformed colored man. Thus Wright invokes criticism of radicals and liberals, Communist and otherwise, as he exhibits a growing distrust of the possibility for interracial political cooperation.

Jan and Mary are both guilty of wanting to wave a magic wand and change America. No matter how altruistic such a desire might be, it erases or overrides anything that the person identified as the outsider might want.

> "I didn't want [Mrs. Dalton] to find me there [in Mary's bedroom]. Well, the girl was trying to say something and I was scared. I just put the edge of the pillow in her mouth and. . . . I didn't mean to kill her. I just pulled the pillow over her face and she died. Her ma came into the room and the girl was trying to say something and her ma had her hands stretched out, like this, see? I was scared she was going to touch me. I just sort of pushed the pillow hard over the girl's face to keep her from yelling. Her ma didn't touch me; I got out of the way. But when she left I went to the bed and the girl. . . . She. . . . She was dead. . . . That was all. She was dead. . . . I didn't mean. . . ."[11]

Earlier, when Bigger admits to Bessie that he has killed Mary, he asserts it almost aggressively—"Yeah, I killed the girl"—as he implicates Bessie by suggesting that she is in "as deep" as he is and that she has to help him because she has "spent some of the money." Now, after everything has fallen apart and Bigger is on the run, he gives a more elaborate account of what happened on that fateful evening. Here is a problematic case of guilt declaring innocence or of innocence acknowledging guilt. Bigger accepts responsibility for Mary's death, but . . . he doesn't accept responsibility for her death. "I didn't mean" exhibits the innocence; "She was dead" marks the guilt. This is probably the most meaningful and gentle exchange that Bigger has with Bessie—or with any other character except perhaps Max—and the most remorseful (if we can call this remorse) expression he utters for what he has done. There is almost a softness here that does not exist elsewhere. His halting account of what happened and his repeated "I didn't mean to" will echo through the remainder of the text. His final transformation will occur when he owns, thoroughly, his "I didn't mean to."[12]

Here, he wants Bessie to identify with his fear, to understand that, instead of having evil intentions, he was forced into a situation over which he had no control.[13] His programmed reaction, he wants her to understand, has been bred into him by the racist American society in which they both live. No young Black man in such a compromised position with a young white woman can be innocent, he hopes Bessie will understand, so he tries to change the situation. Unfortunately, he smothers Mary to death. Note how he dramatizes the events for Bessie ("like this, see?") and how he just "sort of pushed the pillow hard over the girl's face." He wants Bessie—and by implication readers—to understand that he is fearfully guilty instead of viciously guilty. He urges Bessie to understand the meaning of Mrs. Dalton's appearance in the room—that there could be no claim to innocence. As he almost tenderly describes his actions to Bessie, the fear and emotion of that moment get transformed into what he hopes will not reap rejection from her. Ironically, his telling Bessie the truth and her ultimate response to it (that she does not want to be a part of Bigger's madness) finally lead to his decision that he cannot take her with him and he cannot leave her behind. This moment of sharing, however, is one of the rare instances in which Bigger pauses long enough to answer a question thoroughly—even as readers realize that he may be telling the truth in order to bind Bessie closer to him in his plan for escape. After his revelation, she still refers to him as "Honey," which means that his truth-telling has not, in this moment, elicited total rejection from her. That rejection will develop moments later when a crying Bessie insists that they will be caught and that she does not care what happens. Her response makes her a physical as well as a psychological burden to Bigger, and it paves the way for his rape and murder of her.

In addition, Bigger distances himself emotionally from Mary, which in turn distances him from his action. He refers to Mary four times as "the girl," thus depersonalizing her and not enabling the specificity of her name to deepen his responsibility or to frighten Bessie even more. Pronoun references enhance that distancing. By attempting to make Mary disappear, Bigger thus pushes her to the side of ownership for her death. He thereby deprives her of specific individuality; she is just some generalized body that happened to be between his desire not to be discovered and Mrs. Dalton's entrance into Mary's bedroom. By depersonalizing Mary and therefore keeping her at arm's length from himself as well as from Bessie, he strategizes linguistically to soften what he has done physically. If he can make Mary less real to Bessie, then perhaps his killing Mary will not seem so horrible to Bessie—and ultimately, to himself.

"I want to read the paper." "Say, can I see a paper?"[14]

Bigger's Fate is to be on display, à la Ota Benga or some other monstrous manifestation of Black abnormality or monstrosity. The eager mob outside the jailhouse, the passion-inciting Buckley, and the distorted newspaper coverage combine to suggest that civilization has passed Bigger by, that he is some kind of neanderthal throwback. Yet Bigger is like a moth drawn to a flame; he wants to read how he is portrayed. Having risen from the faceless masses of Black people to the focus of an entire city—and perhaps an entire nation—Bigger cannot resist reading about his "accomplishments." Is there some perverted pride in his desire to read about his own dehumanization? Recall his reaction when Buckley suggests that Jan either wrote the kidnap note or told Bigger to write it because, Buckley believes, Bigger is incapable of such intellectual deviousness. Bigger resists the implication; he perceives that

Buckley is attempting to take something from him. No matter how atrocious the acts he has committed, they still belong *exclusively* to him, and he embraces that claiming. Newspapers become, then, somewhat of a mirror for Bigger as well as a carnival house of mirroring distortions that challenge his perceptions of self.

The newspapers are also a form of opiate for Bigger. When he reads about himself, his deeds are constantly ongoing, whereas he himself is locked away. With the newspapers, he is always in action, which means that it is almost like watching a movie of himself, one that keeps repeating reel after reel after reel. From his jail cell, he is metaphorically in a movie theater, seeing images and narratives about himself unfold before his very eyes. His reading might border on narcissism, but that is not the whole story. Bigger is reading to see how he is created in the public imagination, how his invisibility becomes visible. It does not matter that the attention is name-calling, ugly, and negative. It is still attention, and he is the person who has generated that attention. Even when he disagrees or becomes disgusted with the portrayals, he nonetheless reads, for he is the subject on which many folks have focused, and he finds their narratives engaging, no matter how ugly. He has commanded the time and energy of scores of people, and they in turn have provided him with a satisfying concoction of pictures and stories. He may put the papers down for a time, but he never fails to return to them, for the perverted affirmation they offer nonetheless confirms his existence.

"I can die without a cross!"[15]

As with the declaration that he *could* fly a plane if he were allowed to do so, Bigger declares that he does not need religion to accompany him to death. This is bravado, as the exclamation point might suggest, but it is also the final intersection of Wright's and

Bigger's viewpoints, Job notwithstanding. Bigger has witnessed how the Ku Klux Klan uses the cross, the same symbol his mother has given him, to suggest a lynching/burning that they would like to bestow upon him. If the so-called goodness of the cross cannot be separated from the murderous intentions of the Klan and other mobsters, then Bigger wants nothing to do with it. Just as he has explained earlier that he left church because it provided no concrete way to deal with his poverty-stricken life, so now he rejects the symbol of that church and the acquiescence it engenders. Declaring that he can die without a cross allows Bigger to claim the individuality toward which he has been working for the entire "Fate" section of the novel. He realizes, as Donald B. Gibson argues so eloquently, that he can depend only upon himself and the growth he exhibits as a result of self-examination.[16] To embrace the cross and religion at this point would be to latch on to his mother's crutch (comparable to Bessie's alcohol, he argues). If he must be existentially alone at this point, then that is how he will be. He will not fall back on a folk religion that, from his perspective, has done little for the masses of Black people and definitely nothing for him.[17]

Worthy of note is that the primary messenger of Christianity, Reverend Hammond, is an illiterate and ineffective minister who harks back to Wright's earlier portraits of such characters in works like "Big Boy Leaves Home." If ever an instance of self-presentation ensures that a message will be rejected, then Reverend Hammond's inadvertently negative performance fits that bill. His speech is caricature. Wright even portrays the uneducated, twenty-year-old Bigger as possessing a better command of the English language than Reverend Hammond. And while readers can certainly argue that books should not be judged by their covers, Reverend Hammond offers little in the way of refutation for such an assessment. His theology is simplistic, inherited, unexamined. Bigger knew as an adolescent that he did not want to embrace what Reverend Hammond espouses, and he has not changed his mind. Wright's rejection of Christianity gets manifested in his portrayal of Reverend Hammond, which in turn leads Bigger to conclude that his own rejection of Christianity is the correct path.

> "*Like* her? I *hated* her! So help me God, I hated her! . . . She asked me a
> lot of questions. She acted and talked in a way that made me hate her.
> She made me feel like a dog. I was so mad I wanted to cry. . . ."[18]

Finally, Bigger is able to articulate his feelings about Mary to Max. In her presence, he can only register discomfort and *think* what he feels about Mary. Here, he expresses the hatred that undergirded his discomfort. By moving from feeling to verbalization, Bigger again reveals his understanding of the system of oppression that resulted in her death. Mary's attempt at friendliness, in what has amounted to cultural voyeurism, has only served to make Bigger feel even more acutely the distance between them. Mary is white; Bigger is Black; Mary is rich; Bigger is not. Custom and law in 1930s America dictated that the twain should not meet except in employer-to-servant relationships. Bigger has no script to respond when a white person, especially a white woman, deviates from that pattern. It only leads him to feel more dehumanized—"like a dog." The dog imagery is one that Wright resorts to on several occasions in his works and in his autobiography. In *Black Boy,* for instance, he recounts how white men at the factory where he worked in Memphis forced him and another young Black man to fight. He told the other young man: "I don't want to fight for white men. I'm no dog or rooster." Yet, the white men build up such distrust between the two young Black males that they end up fighting each other so brutally that they can never again interact pleasantly. Bigger is forced to continue to interact with Mary and Jan despite the subhuman category Mary forces him into with her blatant curiosity, which constitutes a kind of rape (relentless prying and penetration into the life of someone she perceives as outside her realm of existence).[19]

The utter control Mary exhibits with Bigger, whether she intends it or not, casts her as violating the spatial dynamics that control Black and white social interactions. By insisting that Bigger ride in the front seat of the car with her and Jan, Mary has abandoned the pedestal to which history has consigned white women. By further insisting that Bigger eat with her and Jan, Mary is similarly out of place. However, as a white woman in America, Mary is simultaneously and paradoxically "in place" wherever she chooses to be. She can violate unspoken rules that Bigger does not dare to violate. Her white privilege thus places Bigger in an untenable situation where his only reaction is rage. If only Mary would behave as a white woman is expected to in 1930s America, Bigger thinks, then there would be no problem. By ignoring custom, by defining her place as wherever she wants it to be—that is, by her flaunted whiteness—Mary inadvertently evokes in Bigger the hatred he expresses to Max. Again, Bigger has no script for responding to an "out-of-place-though-in-place-wherever-she-wants-to-be-white-woman." Mary's prying questions, together with her bodily, physical, and social violations of space, place her in danger without her realizing it and evoke in Bigger an inarticulate rage that makes him want to cry. Being put in the position of wanting to cry, even if no tears are shed, is emasculating for Bigger, and therefore his animosity toward Mary and hatred of her can only increase.

"They kill you before you die."[20]

How does one respond to the glitter and glamor of American life being dangled before one's face every day, every hour of the day, with the knowledge that it is always beyond one's reach? To Bigger and his friends, America is like the movies to which they are drawn. They can watch, but they can never enter the white house of America and acquire all the things that they witness from the outside. Their hopes and aspirations are killed before they are born. They must either adjust their expectations or beat their heads bloody against walls that they can never break down. They die metaphorically, therefore, each time they are rejected for jobs, each time they are refused admission to school, each time they want to take a girlfriend out for dinner and a movie and do not have the funds to do so. They die each time they watch young white men their age go to work as executives in banks or in companies where the Black males must go to seek jobs as janitors or elevator operators. They die each time they think on the fact that, as long as they live in America and conditions are what they are, they will never be a part of the country they call home. Again, that ubiquitous "they" kill them emotionally, psychologically, and, finally, physically. Without access to opportunity, permanently shut out of the power brokering that rules America, and locked away in living quarters where rats stride at will, Bigger and those like him watch themselves as hope dies, as potential altruism turns to criminality, and as whatever expectations they had for a reasonably decent existence come tumbling down around their heads. As Baldwin declares of young Black males who grow up in Harlem without the possibility of healthy futures, who mostly end up drug addicts, criminals, or dead, "their heads bumped abruptly against the low ceiling of their actual possibilities. They were filled with rage."[21]

Bigger is a "boy" in a society ruled by men, and how that society treats "boys" reduces them to sub-humanity, kills them over and over again. Characters use the word "boy" dozens upon dozens of times. It is especially noteworthy with Buckley, but it appears again and again, even in Max's defense of Bigger.[22] "Boy" saps individuality and reduces Bigger and other young Black males to faceless blobs that warrant, as far as the labelers are concerned, no consideration from society. Boys are blamed for their own conditions, so these keepers of language maintain, and all Black boys have a tendency to do evil. (Remember the southern sheriff's comment about the evilness of a six-year-old Black male, in Robert Nixon's case.) Black boys are pushed behind the fence of racism through which they can see America only via knot-hole, and narratives about them ensure that, if they should escape their caged positions, they will be destroyed. The boy-ness imposed upon Black males makes their lives a living death, and, unless they act out criminally, as Bigger does, they will move through life in zombie-like states controlled by the racist forces of American society.

> "Well, to tell the truth, Mr. Max, it seems sort of natural-like, me being here facing that death chair. Now I come to think of it, it seems like something like this just had to be."[23]

Inevitably, Bigger moves toward accepting the consequences of his criminal actions. His existence has been prescribed, mathematically formulated so that only certain outcomes are available. He can turn into an acquiescing contemporary Uncle Tom by accepting a job at the lowest rungs of society and becoming complicit in his own degradation, he can become a criminal in petty ways (as he has done in stealing items from the homes where Bessie works), or he can commit murder, which has brought him to death row. The naturalistic path on which Wright has put him has ensured that Bigger ends up precisely where he is. If America is to change, then it must realize the role it has played in bringing Bigger to this outcome.

Though Bigger has also made some choices along the way that

have moved this outcome along, perhaps *any* choice he makes in this controlling environment will yield the same result. He can either be the zombie-like automaton, or he can claim responsibility for his actions. The complexity of choices not leading to any positive outcome versus being totally driven by environment and socioeconomic conditions make inevitability the end result, no matter which interpretive posture gets selected. As Bigger has experienced his limitations, watched his life devolve in comparison to what America presumably promises its citizens, and been cornered by his own personal demons, it is indeed "natural-like" that he ends up where he is.

Nonetheless, readers will recall that many characters in the novel, including Bigger's family and his friends, do not end in the same "natural-like," life-ending set of circumstances. They, like the caged birds of Paul Laurence Dunbar and Maya Angelou, have managed to negotiate their confinements. They may not have done so with much success, but they have been able to combat the "naturalness" to destruction that Bigger claims defines his existence. In contrast to those who were willing to settle for their lot in life, Bigger dares to dream; it is that daring, no matter how minuscule, that distinguishes him from the masses around him. Bigger's intentional unintentional choices have led him to the point at which he utters this. Things he could have done better (how he treated his family, his friends, and Bessie) do not register at this point. He lapses into blaming forces that are beyond his control, to repositioning himself as a victim of a world that shows him no mercy and no pity.

> "But when I think of why all the killing was, I begin to feel what I wanted, what I am. . . . I didn't want to kill! . . . But what I killed for, I *am!* It must've been pretty deep in me to make me kill! I must have felt it awful hard to murder. . . ."[24]

Bigger's pathway to inevitability ends on death row and his final conversation with Max. And mercy and pity are not what Bigger wants at this point. In this often-quoted passage, Bigger claims what he has done and declares its ability to define him. Max is horrified, and many readers are appalled. Nonetheless, as those readers have agreed to read, to go on this journey with Bigger, they are obliged to hear what Bigger has to say about where he is. The up-by-the-bootstraps tradition of American striving presumably enables citizens to carve out their fortune-making identities. Bigger's identity, his negative fortune, is irrevocably linked to his killing of Mary and his murder of Bessie. He cannot erase the past, but he can try to understand what has happened to him, why he has done what he has done. As the scholar Donald Gibson points out, the "Fate" section of the novel moves from social issues to existential ones. Bigger recognizes that he is now outside the social structure in a different way. There is no longer any reason to contemplate success or failure in that realm. What he now contemplates is where he fits in the grand scheme of things as an individual human being who has taken life from other human beings. Humanity outside of social structures, humanity outside of class structure, humanity outside of racial structures: these are the things on which he finally focuses.[25]

If his killing has indeed transformed his sense of identity, then there must have been something good in what he did—no matter its destructiveness and violation of social contracts. When all is stripped away, when Bigger must confront himself for the possible monster that society deems him to be, he can look long, hard, and coolly into himself and conclude that there is no distinction between who he is and what he has done. He has arrived at a place of contentment not unlike the state Jefferson achieves in Ernest J. Gaines's *A Lesson Before Dying* (1993). Falsely accused of a killing and sentenced to death, Jefferson contemplates his situation extensively.

Although he is innocent and Bigger is guilty, society treats both the same way. The only viable option for either is to rise above the dehumanizing labels that others apply to them (Jefferson is called a hog, and Bigger is compared to various animals) and try to understand themselves and accept who they are before they exit the world. Bigger may shock Max, who, as many scholars have pointed out, sees Bigger more as a symbol of the working classes than as a human being, but he does not shock himself or sensitive readers. Bigger is "nobody but himself," and in his declaration of "selfness" against forces that would destroy that self, he anticipates two of his literary sons who arrived at similar conclusions. He is who he is as assuredly as Ellison's narrator and Jim Trueblood echoed the sentiment twelve years later. "I yam what I yam," declares the narrator as he tries to reconcile his southern background with his northern opportunities. After having raped and impregnated his daughter, who is pregnant at the same time as her mother, Trueblood concludes, against the cacophony of critics who maintain that he is monstrous, that "All I know is I *ends up* singin' the blues. I sings me some blues that night ain't never been sang before, and while I'm singin' them blues I makes up my mind that I ain't nobody but myself and ain't nothin' I can do but let whatever is gonna happen, happen."[26]

The pathway to his recognition, Trueblood maintains, is the blues. By embracing that condition and singing the songs that define it, Trueblood transcends tragedy and declares victory. So, too, with Bigger. He may not label his condition in the way that Trueblood does, but the condition predates the labeling. Bigger's entire life has been a state of the blues, which is again ironic given the accusations that Wright did not respect or embrace the African American folk tradition.[27] Bigger is a living example of the blues. His being outside that tradition does not enable him to label what troubles him as such, but the condition nonetheless exists. With his blues—no job, no opportunity to fly, no consistent ability to help his family, resorting to petty and then major crime—and no viable way of expressing them, Bigger is an inchoate mass without a creative outlet. Like Toni Morrison's Sula, his literary grand-daughter, he has no paints or crayons into which to pour a poten-tial creative energy that otherwise manifests in destructive choices. His blues condition only finds expression in voicing to Max, but Max is incapable of understanding. It is left to readers to mark and reflect upon Bigger's blues and to understand that he has arrived at the most viable state possible for his condition and his life. Big-ger is a victim and a victimizer. Conversations have gone on for decades about which is more egregious. They will undoubtedly continue.

CHAPTER 7

————

The Value of a Literary Life

I N 2024, Richard Wright's *Native Son* turned eighty-four years old. Bigger Thomas, however, remains twenty years old. What has it meant to have Bigger in the world during these eight-plus decades? What cultural work has he done? How has that cultural work been manifested in the social realm? How has it been manifested in cultural realms, literary and otherwise? What other arenas have enabled evocations of Bigger? On the landscape of his creation, Bigger has been a touchstone for readers, scholars and critics, movie makers, public policy officials, and the general reading public. He enables continuing insight into the contradictions in American democracy: its gaps, lapses, and exclusions. He continues to evoke debates that have the impact of social and legal conditions as their bases, as well as debates about portrayals of female characters. Issues of morality continue to inform his life, as scholars and others consider ongoing questions of victimization and retaliation for victimization, which in some ways echo the contemporary focus on bullying and its effects on those bullied. Bigger shocked the world in 1940, and he still has the capacity for such shocking in the twenty-first century.

On three occasions—1951, 1986, and 2019—filmmakers have tried to bring Bigger's complicated personality to life on celluloid. According to *The Richard Wright Encyclopedia* (2008), edited by Jerry W. Ward, Jr., and Robert J. Butler, there had been two films made of *Native Son* to that point and they were both "deeply flawed."[1] HBO filmed *Native Son* yet again in 2019. All three attempts fall short of reaching the complexity of character and motivation that defines the novel. From the 1951 film (made in Argentina), with a middle-aged Richard Wright playing the role of Bigger, to the 2019 film, in which Bigger, now reduced to "Big," voices over the action, the films highlight the difficulty of bringing literary texts to the screen. The appeal of such transformation nonetheless remains, which is again a testament to Bigger's long life, but the attempts at realization have consistently resulted in distorted, inept creations. Bigger thus becomes a specific instance of a larger issue that filmmakers, directors, producers, film scholars, and others have tackled for generations. Geography, politics, technology, and generally changing social times all have an impact on how a literary character might appear on screen. Just as Bigger encountered different responses at different periods in literary history and scholarly interpretation, so the same might be said of the circumstances that influence filming.

Despite their lacks, the films might have earned support from Wright, for almost as soon as *Native Son* was published he chased the possibility of making a film of the novel. His collaboration with a French producer resulted in his being cast as Bigger in the 1951 film, which introduced another issue in translating the character to screen, that of age, for Wright was more than forty years old at the time. His portrayal represents the intensity of his desire to have Bigger appear on screen, and that desire is mirrored in the attempts that followed the first film. The 1986 and 2019 versions are a measure of the long-standing impact of the novel on American popular culture, which again makes clear the cultural work that Wright designed Bigger to accomplish. From minimizing the sexual history that informs the interactions between Bigger and Mary to attempts to downplay graphic racism, to incorporation of contemporary technological developments (cell phones, wi-fi) and politics (photographs of President Bill Clinton and Supreme Court justice Sonia Sotomayor), to attempts at racial liberalism and diversity, the later films try to adjust the novel to their contemporary moments. In addition to toning down racism, Bigger's violence is softened, fewer policemen are involved in chasing him, and, in the most recent film, Bessie and Mary are almost equalized, in that both are college students. Such changes reflect the constant challenges of bringing to life a literary text that has been composed in a particular historical moment. "Modernizing" the text is just as difficult as capturing the essence of the character.[2]

Bigger's social cultural contributions began in the immediate aftermath of the publishing of *Native Son*. Public policy officials, policemen, and other city personnel in the Chicago area read the novel and used it as the basis for discussions about how the lives of young Black people in the area could be improved. Bigger became the exemplar for what needed to be changed in programming for young Black people and otherwise altering the negative life trajectories predicted for them. In the twenty-first century, Bigger Thomas is Trayvon Martin. Bigger Thomas is Michael Brown. Bigger Thomas is George Floyd. Granted, these young Black men did not commit crimes as Bigger did. What connects them to Bigger is their Blackness, their expendability, and their lack of value in American society. Bigger was devalued and dismissed *long before* he killed Mary and murdered Bessie. He, like these young Black men in the twenty-first century, was killed before he died. An outsider status thus inhabits them as assuredly as it prevailed with Bigger in the 1930s. Bigger Thomas is, as Wright predicted, multiplied millions of times over in places where racism, economics, and the general failures of American democracy hold sway.

Bigger's relevance to the social circumstances of contemporary American society has engaged the scholarly focus of Thabiti Lewis, who sees Bigger reincarnated in Michael Brown. "A structure that situates Mike Brown as a 21st century reality of fictional Bigger Thomas—a reincarnation—is more accurate assessment and forceful response to the sufferings and aspirations of the black majority in the contemporary moment," Lewis argues. He maintains that Wright's character bears "witness to contemporary extralegal violence and systemic disenfranchisement" of African-descended people in the twenty-first century, that "Mike Brown is a metonym for a new Bigger only more petrifying," and that "Wright remains a beacon for contextualizing and particularizing truth in the 21st century." Lewis's wrenching meditation on Brown and all that he means for contemporary politics and race is a striking example of how scholarship intersects with activism in African American literary studies as it particularizes the impact of Bigger and his contemporary significance.[3]

Since Bigger's life is set in Chicago, it is instructive to consider what twenty-first-century crime and incarceration rates are for young Black men in that area and for Black males generally. Research that Michelle Alexander conducted for *The New Jim Crow: Mass Incarceration in the Age of Colorblindness* (2012) revealed that fifty-five percent of Black males in Chicago had a felony record. Between 1985 and 2005, the rate of incarceration of Black males for drug crimes increased by two thousand percent. Alexander provides startling projected and current statistics: "One in three young African American men will serve time in prison if current trends continue, and in some cities more than half of all young adult black men are currently under correctional control—in prison or jail, on probation or parole." Just as Bigger Thomas and Robert

Nixon were caught in the legal system in the 1930s, so young Black males in the twenty-first century are caught. Innocence or guilt gets pushed into the background in the face of systemic racial inequality and the supra-representation of Black males in jails and prisons, on parole or probation, or who otherwise have their lives altered permanently by encounters with the American legal system.[4]

Bigger Thomas is therefore more disposable Black men than the society is willing to admit it has. Each attempt to dispose of him, however, has led to his capturing ever more deeply the American imagination. For example, #BlackLivesMatter and all the other "remember this young Black man" memorials that have occurred because some young Black man died, innocently or otherwise, constantly evoke comparison to Bigger. Bigger "calls" to activists in the twenty-first century, and, whether they are at their desks or in their political offices or on the streets, they "respond" to that call. Thus, #BlackLivesMatter constitutes one manifestation of the activist agenda that Wright envisioned for incorporating African-descended people into American democracy.[5]

In addition, Bigger's literary cultural contributions have been on the international stage. Every time a conference has been held in another country on Wright, or African American literature including presentations on Wright, some scholar has worked on his or her language skills to navigate the selected conference country. Japanese scholars have honed their English language skills to conduct research on Wright's haiku. As scholars have worked across national borders, they in turn have learned more about each other. Collaborations have occurred in publishing books, articles, and special editions of journals. Collaborations have occurred in teaching. The well-known Wright scholars Maryemma Graham and Jerry W. Ward, Jr., for example, have both taught Wright to students in China. Indeed, Ward has collaborated with Chinese scholars generally in the study of African American literature. No matter how strange it may sound, Bigger has served as an ambassador, for he has fostered language learning and international understanding, cooperation, and travel.

Bigger has led to thousands upon thousands of scholars, critics, and readers devoting their time and talents to contemplating his actions and role in *Native Son,* his place in American society, his place in American and African American literary studies. He has inspired these critics and scholars to spend their brilliance on him, and he has rewarded them with the creation of a body of scholarship that will stand for generations. Literary lives create literary scholars—and countless scholars have earned their reputations writing about Wright and Bigger. Even the quickest glance at Wright scholarship will reveal the extent to which some scholars, such as Keneth Kinnamon and Robert J. Butler, have built their scholarly reputations mostly upon work on Wright and Bigger. These scholars and others have in turn assured that Bigger remains a part of English and other department curricula as they have taught undergraduate and graduate courses, and directed countless undergraduate honors theses, master's theses, and doctoral dissertations on Wright. A brief internet search for *Native Son* yields nearly four hundred thousand items, which are surely a testament to Bigger's ongoing cultural significance. Responses to Bigger have provided a way to measure scholarly trends and to note the evolution of the enterprise of literary scholarly studies.

Wright scholars have shaped the trajectory of criticism on Bigger for the past eighty-four years. Although that criticism has changed with political and social times and movements, such as the Black Arts Movement and feminist perspectives, making it softer here, harder there, Bigger never changes. He is always already there as Wright presented him to the world in 1940. Scholarship about him has run the gamut from thematic to historical to sociological to theoretical approaches, and it evolves constantly. As new critical approaches become available to scholars, they in turn will apply them to Bigger. (It will be fascinating to see when the Afrofuturist trend hits Bigger!) In the meantime, Bigger will always greet readers and scholars by being perpetually engaging, racially astute, and permanently flawed. His killings have not led to his erasure from the American literary canon just as his guilt has not led to such erasure. Instead, his actions have guaranteed his inclusion, and have extended his already long life.

In the history of African American literature, various characters have committed actions that might evoke comparison to Bigger, but perhaps only one other work has approximated the kind of reader and critical response that *Native Son* received: *The Color Purple*, by Alice Walker (1982). In this book, as with *Native Son*, the actions of a male character outraged and offended many readers. Although "Mr." does not kill Celie or anyone else, his domination and repression of Celie, his stilling of her voice, and his emotional browbeating of her evoke deeply negative responses from readers. In the feminist era of Walker's creation of Celie, domestic violence equates powerfully with murder. Celie fits easily into Bigger's observation that "they kill you before you die." Mr. assumes the role of violent repressor comparable to what Bigger does with Bessie. In microcosmic representation, Bigger and Mr. become, in their treatment of Bessie and Celie, smaller versions of what the larger society does to Bigger, Mr., and Black people in general. Fortunately, Celie rises from her zombie-like state and escapes Mr.'s abuse. The responses to Walker's novel were a direct result of the impact of the feminist movement and illustrate yet again how the social and cultural politics of a particular time period shape critical and scholarly responses to fictional works. Mr., as Bigger's grandson, may not be quite as physically violent as Bigger, but his emotional violence goes on for years. In making comparisons between the two characters, therefore, intensity and duration of impacts they have upon characters around them are just as significant as what they actually do. Bigger kills in two heightened, compressed moments of his life; Mr. tortures Celie emotionally and brutalizes her physically for years. Mr. is finally redeemed, but Bigger is not. Yet Mr., like his grandfather Bigger, lives on in American literary studies, serving as a contemporary example of the complexity of such characters as readers and scholars focus interpretive attention on them.

Bigger, the killer outsider, lives on with Mr. as well as with other of his sons (Freeman in Greenlee's *The Spook Who Sat by the Door*) and grandsons (Kenyatta in Donald Goines's *Death List*). Their literary immortality showcases the power of literary creation, at which Wright was masterful. As he waited anxiously for word that *Native Son* would indeed be published, Wright had no idea how popular his novel would become or how long readers and scholars would focus on it. What was clear to him was that he would do all he could to ensure that his child entered the world, survived, and thrived. Bigger has far exceeded Wright's expectations. He has become inseparable from the study of American and African American literature. His literary life makes clear the complexities of reading and interpretation, the impact of history, the power of tradition, and the realization of one writer's finest dream.

ACKNOWLEDGMENTS

———

As always, I am grateful to the many people who made another of my scholarly projects possible. I begin by thanking Henry Louis Gates, Jr. His invitation to consider writing a book for the Black Lives Series at Yale University Press inspired me to conceptualize a biography of Bigger Thomas.

I am especially thankful to my sister, Anna Harris McCarthy, who is an untiring and generous reader and always provides welcome feedback. The scholars and creative writers who make up the Wintergreen Women Writers' Collective, of which I was a founding member thirty-six years ago, are still consistently a source of inspiration and encouragement. In this instance, I am grateful to one of our number, Ethel Morgan Smith, who took the time to read the manuscript and offer invaluable commentary.

Thanks to all the wonderful people who attended my Retirement Reception at the Dinah Washington Cultural Arts Center in Tuscaloosa, Alabama, on May 4, 2022, and expressed enthusiasm and encouragement when I told them about this project. Thanks, everyone! I hope you enjoy the result.

Ushering a book through the publication process takes incredible amounts of time and energy. I am indebted to Jessie Kindig for her close reading and editorial suggestions. The book is much better because it has the benefit of her skills. I also express appreciation to Ash Lago for providing advice on securing permissions for the book. Thanks, as well, to Phillip King for taking the book through the production process.

I thank Cynthia Landeen, my indexer, who, yet again, has ensured that I "like the way my book ends."

NOTES

Introduction

1. Readers and scholars cannot help but note that Wright's selection of the name "Bigger" for his major character rhymes with the word "nigger," the historically derogatory term for African-descended people in the United States. Bigger thus evokes the devaluing and diminishing of Black people in America, and that history of racism undergirds all of his actions even as it implicitly informs reader response to the character.

2. For his take on the impact of kitchenette buildings on Black lives, see Richard Wright, *12 Million Black Voices: A Folk History of the Negro in the United States* (Brattleboro, Vt.: Echo Point Books & Media, 2019; originally published in 1941).

3. Richard Wright, *Native Son* (New York: HarperPerennial, 1993; originally published in 1940), 310. Wright does not reconcile the seeming contradiction between Mrs. Thomas having sufficient water in her "apartment" to do laundry for whites while she and her family do not take showers or baths before dressing. As noted, bathrooms were usually shared among tenants in kitchenette buildings. Indeed, in her poem "kitchenette building" (1963), Gwendolyn Brooks depicts how her speaker has many dreams but must face the reality of getting into the bathroom down the hall while the water is still "lukewarm"; Gwendolyn Brooks, *Selected Poems* (New York: HarperPerennial, 2006), 3.

4. Details covered in the preceding several paragraphs about Wright's life in Mississippi, Arkansas, and Memphis can be gleaned easily from his first autobiography, *Black Boy* (New York: Perennial, 1966; originally published in 1945), as well as from biographies of him, including Michel Fabre, *The Unfinished Quest of Richard Wright* (Urbana: University of Illinois Press, 1993), and Hazel Rowley,

Richard Wright: The Life and Times (Chicago: University of Chicago Press, 2010). Scholars such as Keneth Kinnamon also provide details of Wright's early life, as in Keneth Kinnamon, "*Native Son:* The Personal, Social, and Political Background," *Phylon* 30, no. 1 (1st qtr., 1969): 66–72.

5. Margaret Walker, *Richard Wright: Daemonic Genius: A Portrait of the Man, a Critical Look at His Work* (New York: Warner, 1988), 73–74.

6. Zora Neale Hurston, "What White Publishers Won't Print," in *I Love Myself When I Am Laughing . . . And Then Again When I Am Looking Mean and Impressive,* ed. Alice Walker (New York: Feminist Press, 1988), 169–73.

7. Sterling Brown, "The Literary Scene," *Opportunity* 26 (April 1938): 120–21.

8. Walker, *Richard Wright,* 149.

CHAPTER 1. The Birth of Bigger Thomas

1. Richard Wright, "Between the World and Me," *Partisan Review* (1935). The poem inspired Ta-Nehisi Coates's *Between the World and Me: Notes on the First 150 Years in America* (New York: Spiegel and Grau, 2015).

2. Michel Fabre, *The Unfinished Quest of Richard Wright* (Urbana: University of Illinois Press, 1993), 188; Richard Wright, "Blueprint for Negro Writing," *New Challenge* (Autumn 1937).

3. His biographer Fabre describes Wright as one of the "literary stars" of the Communist Party during this period, who "attended various political functions and activities as a result"; Fabre, *Unfinished Quest of Richard Wright,* 162.

4. Wright lifted the name "Mary Dalton" from the radical female Communist who had been involved in a case referenced as the "Atlanta Six." For comments on this case and Wright's intentionally humorous incorporation of the name, see Rowley, *Richard Wright,* 155. Keneth Kinnamon points out that the Mary Dalton scene was inspired by an incident that occurred when Wright worked on a job as a fifteen-year-old for a family by the name of Bibb: "his duties included chopping wood, carrying coal, and tending the fire." The family had a daughter who was kind to Wright "within the limits of Southern custom, but when, on one occasion, he chanced upon her in her bedroom while she was dressing, 'she reprimanded him and told him to knock before entering a room.' The diffident and fearful young Negro handyman, the amiable white girl, the sexually significant situation—these elements, transmuted, found their way into *Native Son.*" Kinnamon, "*Native Son:* The Personal, Social, and Political Background," *Phylon* 30, no. 1 (1st qtr., 1969): 66–67. Kinnamon also recounts this incident in *The Emergence of Richard Wright* (Urbana: University of Illinois Press, 1972), 119–20. The Dalton name is also symbolic. Kinnamon notes: "In the Chi-

cago hospital where he worked, Wright learned of that variety of color blindness called Daltonism"; *Emergence of Richard Wright*, 120.

5. Richard Wright, "How 'Bigger' Was Born," Afterword to *Native Son* (New York: HarperPerennial, 1993), 454.

6. Wright, "How 'Bigger' Was Born," 434, 444.

7. Wright, "How 'Bigger' Was Born," 436, 437.

8. Wright, "How 'Bigger' Was Born," 437.

9. Wright, "How 'Bigger' Was Born," 443.

10. Wright, "How 'Bigger' Was Born," 447–48, 443.

11. Richard Wright, "The Ethics of Living Jim Crow," in *Uncle Tom's Children* (New York: HarperCollins, 1993; originally published in 1940), 11.

12. Wright, "Ethics of Living Jim Crow," 12–13.

13. Trudier Harris, *Exorcising Blackness: Historical and Literary Lynching and Burning Rituals* (Philadelphia: Temple University Press, 1984), 105–9.

14. Space is also relevant in thinking of the actual physical demarcations of the South Side of Chicago. It falls into the category of "shunned space," a concept that Barry M. Cole identifies as geographical areas into which people of color and other minorities have been forced physically, politically, socially, and economically. Inhabitants are disenfranchised and often suffer irreparable damage to their physical health and their emotional, political, economic, and social well-being. Such spaces are sources of scarcity, subject to environmental degradation, and generally susceptible to invasion by the larger society. Barry M. Cole, "Shunned Space Theory as a Holistic Framework for Understanding Characters and Communities in Selected Writings of Jesmyn Ward, Richard Wright, and William Faulkner," Dissertation, Department of English, University of Alabama, 2019.

15. Arna Bontemps's *Black Thunder: Gabriel's Revolt* (1936), based on Gabriel Prosser's planned revolt of enslaved persons in Virginia in 1800, focuses on a desire for freedom and overthrowing the government, but its direct basis in history precludes my consideration of it in relation to Bigger's actions among literary relatives.

16. Wright, "How 'Bigger' Was Born," 449–50; emphasis in original.

17. Wright, "How 'Bigger' Was Born," 453–54. Joseph T. Skerrett, Jr., briefly discusses the impact of Wright's job on the writing of *Native Son* in "Composing Bigger: Wright and the Making of *Native Son*," in *Richard Wright: A Collection of Critical Essays*, ed. Arnold Rampersad (New York: Simon & Schuster, 1995), 26–39.

18. Wright, "How 'Bigger' Was Born," 448.

19. More than one Wright biographer notes several of these facts. However, I am indebted to Michel Fabre for his account of most of the details in this paragraph; Fabre, *Unfinished Quest of Richard Wright*, especially chapters 8 and 9. An

account of the Book-of-the-Month Club sales appears in the same Fabre work at page 557, note 13.

20. Keneth Kinnamon, "Introduction," in *New Essays on Native Son*, ed. Keneth Kinnamon (Cambridge University Press, 1990), 18.

21. Rowley, *Richard Wright*, 165.

22. Kinnamon observes, appropriately, that Fisher's Introduction "is a latter-day example of the process of white authentication which Robert Stepto has shown to be so characteristic a feature of slave narratives"; Kinnamon, "Introduction," 17.

23. Rowley, *Richard Wright*, 183. Rowley offers extended commentary on the changes to the novel, at pages 181–85. For more commentary on the changes made to *Native Son*, see Arnold Rampersad, "Too Honest for His Own Time," *New York Times Book Review*, December 29, 1991, 3.

24. Rowley, *Richard Wright*, 183; Rampersad, "Too Honest," 3. For detailed commentary on the changes Wright was asked to make to *Native Son*, see Kinnamon, "Introduction," and Laurence Cossu-Beaumont, "Richard Wright and His Editors: A Work Under the Influence? From the Signifyin(g) Rebel to the Exiled Intellectual," in *Richard Wright in a Post-Racial Imaginary*, ed. Alice Mikal Craven and William E. Dow (London: Bloomsbury, 2014), 83–97. Cossu-Beaumont also discusses changes the Book-of-the-Month Club forced Wright to make to *Black Boy* (1945), which it also selected. Fisher played an even more prominent role in the revisions the club requested to Wright's autobiography.

CHAPTER 2. Of Men and Monsters

1. Richard Wright, "Blueprint for Negro Writing," in *Richard Wright Reader*, ed. Ellen Wright and Michel Fabre (New York: Harper & Row, 1978), 47–48.

2. Wright, "Blueprint for Negro Writing," 48.

3. W. E. B. Du Bois, "Criteria of Negro Art," in *Within the Circle: An Anthology of African American Literary Criticism from the Harlem Renaissance to the Present*, ed. Angelyn Mitchell (Durham: Duke University Press, 1994), 66, 67; James Weldon Johnson, "Preface" to *The Book of American Negro Poetry* (New York: Harcourt Brace Jovanovich, 1959), 9.

4. Johnson, "Preface," 41, 42; emphasis in original.

5. Countee Cullen, "Incident," in *Black Writers of America: A Comprehensive Anthology*, ed. Richard Barksdale and Keneth Kinnamon (New York: Macmillan, 1972), 7–8, 9–12.

6. John Hope Franklin and Alfred A. Moss, Jr., *From Slavery to Freedom: A History of African Americans*, 7th edition (New York: Alfred A. Knopf, 1994), 401.

7. Douglas A. Blackmon, *Slavery by Another Name: The Re-Enslavement of*

Black Americans from the Civil War to World War II (New York: Anchor Books, 2008), 310–23. The Pulitzer Prize–winning playwright August Wilson documents the historical practice of jailing innocent Black men in his play *Joe Turner's Come and Gone,* a practice that he locates in Tennessee.

8. Mary S. Bedell, "Employment and Income of Negro Workers—1940–52," *Monthly Labor Review,* June 1953, 598; see also *Negroes in the United States: Their Employment and Economic Status,* Bulletin No. 1119, United States Department of Labor, December 1952; Lorraine Hansberry, *A Raisin in the Sun* (New York: Signet, 1988; originally published in 1959), 73.

9. Wright, *Black Boy,* 284. Isabel Wilkerson lifted Wright's phrase "the warmth of other suns" to use as the title of her exceptionally well received study of African American movement to the North during the Great Migration; Isabel Wilkerson, *The Warmth of Other Suns: The Epic Story of America's Great Migration* (New York: Vintage, 2010).

10. Wright, *12 Million Black Voices.*

11. Robert L. Zangrando, *The NAACP Crusade Against Lynching, 1909–1950* (Philadelphia: Temple University Press, 1980), 4. The journalist Ida B. Wells worked diligently to prove that accusations of rape against Black males who were lynched were false; Ida B. Wells, *Southern Horrors: Lynch Law in All Its Phases* and *A Red Record: Tabulated Statistics and Alleged Causes of Lynching in the United States, 1892–1893–1894,* both of which appear in *Selected Works of Ida B. Wells-Barnett,* ed. Trudier Harris (New York: Oxford University Press, 1991). For a more recent historical study of lynching, see W. Fitzhugh Brundage, *Lynching in the New South: Georgia and Virginia, 1880–1930* (Urbana: University of Illinois Press, 1993).

12. Harris, *Exorcising Blackness.* James Weldon Johnson was almost the victim of one of these indiscretions. He went to a park in Jacksonville, Florida, to meet a woman who had come to share an article with him. The streetcar conductor who dropped him off noticed that a Black man had followed a "white" woman into the park near dark. Johnson and his companion were later surrounded by militia, arrested, and taken by streetcar to police headquarters. It was only because Johnson, an attorney newly admitted to the bar, knew the man whose custody he was delivered into that he could explain that the "white" woman was really a very light-skinned Black woman. The possibility of rape loomed in the air, leading Johnson to conclude: "in the core of the heart of the American race problem the sex factor is rooted; rooted so deeply that it is not always recognized when it shows at the surface" (170). To the white males arresting Johnson, the surface optics of the situation were all they needed to almost lynch him. An account of the incident appears in *Along This Way: The Autobiography of James Weldon Johnson* (New York: Viking, 1968; originally published in 1933), 165–70.

13. Zangrando, *The NAACP Crusade*, 4; Harris, *Exorcising Blackness*, x. Douglas Blackmon recounts the instance of a couple of Black males in Alabama who were lynched because they planned "to live like white folks and marry white wives"; Blackmon, *Slavery by Another Name*, 26. If even presumed *thoughts* from African American males could warrant such swift mob reaction, then it is even more the case that swiftness of extermination would come when actual crimes were committed.

14. Harper Lee, *To Kill a Mockingbird* (New York: J. P. Lippincott, 1960).

15. Wright, *Native Son*, 279, 280.

16. Wright, *Native Son*, 281.

17. Wright returned to the concept of outsiders and outsider status in his novel *The Outsider* (New York: Harper & Brothers, 1953). The protagonist, Cross Damon, is an existential outsider who wreaks more havoc than Bigger Thomas could remotely have imagined. Unlike Bigger, Cross is much better equipped intellectually to analyze his position in society and to take deliberate, calculated, and murderous actions to highlight that status.

18. Wright, *Native Son*, 373, 408, 409, 410, 411, 412, 413, 414.

19. Wright, *Native Son*, 331.

20. Claude McKay, *Selected Poems of Claude McKay* (New York: Harvest, 1953), 2, 4, 13–14.

21. For my take on how characters who commit horrible crimes can nonetheless evoke reader sympathy, see "Re-Visiting the Unspeakable: Can Soaphead Church Be Redeemed?" in *The Bloomsbury Handbook to Toni Morrison*, ed. Linda Wagner-Martin and Kelly Reames (London: Bloomsbury, 2023), 31–46.

22. Walker, *Richard Wright*, 122. Another legal case also informed Wright's creation of *Native Son*, especially in the trial scene: that of Nathan Leopold and Richard Loeb, Jewish sons of millionaires in Chicago who, at nineteen and eighteen in 1924, kidnapped and killed Bobby Franks, a fourteen-year-old boy. Their parents hired the attorney Clarence Darrow to defend them, and he succeeded in getting them sentenced to life in prison instead of the electric chair. Robert Butler, "The Loeb and Leopold Case: A Neglected Source for Richard Wright's *Native Son*," *African American Review* 39, no. 4 (Winter 2005): 555–67, details the connections between Max's defense and that of Darrow, concluding, "When arguing their respective clients' motives, Darrow and Max employ similar concepts, words, and phrases" (558). The outcomes differed simply because Leopold and Loeb were white and Bigger was Black. Nonetheless, "By thus connecting Bigger with two other men from vastly different social and economic circumstances, Wright makes an important point about capitalism in America, namely that it corrupted and alienated *all* levels of society, regardless of race and class" (561; emphasis in original).

23. Charles Leavelle, "Brick Slayer Is Likened to Jungle Beast," *Chicago Daily Tribune*, June 5, 1938, 6; Wright, "How 'Bigger' Was Born," 455.

CHAPTER 3. Lightning in a Bottle

1. For a survey of contemporary reactions as well as later reviews of *Native Son*, see Walker, *Richard Wright*, chapter 21, "Fame and Fortune." See also Fabre, *Unfinished Quest of Richard Wright*, chapter 9, Rowley, *Richard Wright*, chapters 10 and 11, and Kinnamon, *Emergence of Richard Wright*, 143–51. For a collection of full text reviews of *Native Son*, see John M. Reilly, ed., *Richard Wright: The Critical Reception* (New York: Burt Franklin, 1978), 38–99. For a succinct coverage of the reviews from 1940, partly geographically based, see Keneth Kinnamon, "Introduction" to *New Essays on Native Son* (Cambridge University Press, 1990), 19–23. A goodly portion of the reviewers compared Wright's novel to Theodore Dreiser's *An American Tragedy* as well as various Dostoyevski works. The Birmingham Public Library stood out in response by banning *Native Son*.

2. Benjamin Davis, Jr., review of *Native Son*, by Richard Wright, *New York Sunday Worker*, April 14, 1940, Section 2, pp. 4, 6; reprinted in Reilly, ed., *Richard Wright*, 69. Limiting the compliment to the year 1940 might in itself be problematic. How many other reputable novels were published that year? And, as a political activist instead of a literary person, how many of them had Davis really kept track of? Wright biographer Addison Gayle labeled Davis's review of *Native Son* "a terrible indictment, striking as severely at the writer's perception of Black life in America as at his indiscretions regarding Marxist aesthetic canons"; Addison Gayle, *Richard Wright: Ordeal of a Native Son* (Garden City, N.Y.: Anchor Press/Doubleday, 1980), 121.

3. Reilly, ed., *Wright: Critical Reception*, 71, 73. Mike Gold, another prominent Communist, was much more positive in his review. See Michael Gold, "Change the World: Dick Wright Gives America a Significant Picture in *Native Son*," review of *Native Son*, by Richard Wright, *Sunday Worker*, March 31, 1940, Section 2, 7.

4. Constance Webb, *Richard Wright: A Biography* (New York: G. P. Putnam's Sons, 1968), 179.

5. Cohn's review is reprinted in Reilly, ed., *Wright: Critical Reception*, 91–93.

6. Being Jewish might also have been a factor in Cohn's castigating Wright and *Native Son*. As a member of a group in America frequently thought of as not white, Cohn might be trying to score points with the white majority by advancing what he believes are its objectives in keeping Blacks subjugated.

7. Richard Wright, "I Bite the Hand That Feeds Me," *Atlantic Monthly* (June 1940), 827; emphasis in original. Wright also could not resist pointing out Bigger's age, which is mentioned on two occasions in the novel, to counter Cohn's claim

that Bigger's "exact age is not stated, but we are told he is too young to vote, and he is therefore under twenty-one"; Reilly, ed., *Wright: Critical Reception*, 91. A cardinal rule for any challenger is to get the facts correct; Cohn's failure to do that simply opened the door wider for Wright's corrective lash.

8. Burton Rascoe, "Negro Novel and White Reviewers," review of *Native Son*, by Richard Wright, *American Mercury* 50 (May 1940): 13–16; reprinted in Reilly, ed., *Wright: Critical Reception*, 88–90.

9. Richard Wright, "Rascoe-Baiting," *American Mercury* 50 (June 1940): 376–77.

10. Burton Rascoe, "Do Critics Help?" *American Mercury* 50 (July 1940): 502–3; Jerry W. Ward, Jr., "Everybody's Protest Novel: The Richard Wright Era," in *The Cambridge Companion to the African American Novel*, ed. Maryemma Graham (Cambridge University Press, 2004), 176.

11. In *A Feeling for Books: The Book-of-the-Month Club, Literary Taste, and Middle-Class Desire* (Chapel Hill: University of North Carolina Press, 1997), Janice A. Radway provides a detailed history of the club, its growth and development, its business practices, and its selection processes and the controversies surrounding them. She mentions briefly the interactions with Richard Wright when the club selected *Native Son* as well as when, a few years later, it selected Wright's autobiography, *Black Boy* (286–87). See also Charles Lee, *The Hidden Public: The Story of the Book-of-the-Month Club* (Garden City, N.Y.: Doubleday, 1958).

12. Dorothy Canfield Fisher, "Introduction" to *Native Son* (New York: Harper & Brothers, 1940), x.

13. The deleted scenes from *Native Son* were restored when the novel was republished by HarperPerennial in 1993, in a volume labeled "The Restored Text Established by The Library of America." See Arnold Rampersad's "Introduction" to the volume as well as "Notes on the Texts" (485–88) and "Notes" (489–504).

14. Walker, *Richard Wright*, 149. Long before her publication of *Richard Wright: Daemonic Genius*, Walker completed an essay on her relationship to Wright; material from that essay was later incorporated into her book. See "Richard Wright," in *Richard Wright: Impressions and Perspectives*, ed. David Ray and Robert M. Farnsworth (Ann Arbor: University of Michigan Press, 1971), 47–67.

15. Walker, *Richard Wright*, 146–47. See also Rowley's comment on Walker's reaction to *Native Son*, in *Richard Wright*, 202. Walker wrote that she read the novel in February 1940; however, the official publication date was March 1, 1940. Walker also refers to Vera as Bigger's "half-sister" rather than his sister.

16. Fabre, *Unfinished Quest of Richard Wright*, 179.

17. Lillian Johnson, "Light and Shadow," review of *Native Son*, by Richard Wright, *Baltimore Afro-American*, April 27, 1940, 13.

18. From unpublished Du Bois papers dated March 6, 1940, quoted in Rowley, *Richard Wright*, 193.

19. One of the criticisms that James Baldwin leveled against the novel a decade later was precisely this lack—that Bigger was cut off from the traditions of African American culture, such as music, that could have sustained him; James Baldwin, "Many Thousands Gone," in *Notes of a Native Son* (New York: Bantam, 1968), 18–36. The essay originally appeared in the *Partisan Review* in 1951.

20. For a discussion of how *King Kong* and other movies and novels, together with Edgar Allan Poe's horror tales, influenced Wright's creation of *Native Son*, see Harold Hellenbrand, "Bigger Thomas Reconsidered: *Native Son*, Film, and *King Kong*," *Journal of American Culture* 6, no. 1 (Spring 1983): 84–95.

21. Early in his long career, Bigger also had a life on the stage. Various advocates, including Orson Welles, John Houseman, Paul Green, Canada Lee (the most famous African American actor of his generation), and Wright himself lobbied to get the novel transformed into a stage play and a film. The stage play, with Lee in the role of Bigger, enjoyed 114 performances on Broadway in 1941 and a touring success after that.

CHAPTER 4. Bigger from the 1950s to the Black Arts Movement

1. R. P. Blackmur, *Language as Gesture: Essays in Poetry* (New York: Harcourt, Brace, 1952), 413, 414. Given the fact that Blackmur makes these comments in the afterword to a volume of essays on American *poets*, his digs at Wright seem especially unwarranted and arrogant, though, in fairness, he also criticizes other fiction writers. From the vantage point of the twenty-first century, scholars have been much more sympathetic in reading Wright's place in the 1950s. See, for example, Ian Afflerbach, "Contemporary Reception," in *Richard Wright in Context*, ed. Michael Nowlin (Cambridge University Press, 2021), 318–28, and Robert J. Butler, "Wright's Critical Reputation, 1960–2019," in *Richard Wright in Context*, ed. Nowlin, 338–47. For an especially careful example of a scholar concentrating on the artistic qualities in *Native Son*, see Joyce Ann Joyce, *Richard Wright's Art of Tragedy* (Iowa City: University of Iowa Press, 1986). See also Joyce Ann Joyce, "Wright's Craft Is as Important as Content in *Native Son*," in Hayley Mitchell, *Readings on Native Son* (San Diego: Greenhaven, 2000), 43–51.

2. See James Baldwin, "Many Thousands Gone," which was republished in *Notes of a Native Son* (New York: Bantam, 1968), 18–36, and Ralph Ellison, "The World and the Jug," in *Shadow and Act* (New York: Signet, 1966), 115–48. As I am sure other scholars have noted, it is truly ironic that Baldwin, who complains

about *Native Son*, would title his collection of essays, obviously evoking Wright, *Notes of a Native Son*.

3. Baldwin, *Notes of a Native Son*, 32. In "Everybody's Protest Novel," Baldwin discusses Harriet Beecher Stowe's *Uncle Tom's Cabin* as a problematic text in the protest tradition and claims that "Bigger is Uncle Tom's descendant" before finally ending the essay by declaring: "The failure of the protest novel lies in its rejection of life, the human being, the denial of his beauty, dread, power, in its insistence that it is his categorization alone which is real and which cannot be transcended" (*Notes of a Native Son*, 17). This essay, which appeared in 1949, was the origin of the rift between Baldwin and Wright. The rift went on for years. Baldwin reflects upon it in "Alas, Poor Richard," one of the essays in *Nobody Knows My Name* (New York: Vintage, 1993; originally published in 1961), 181–215. Baldwin states: "Richard accused me of having betrayed him, and not only him but all American Negroes by attacking the idea of protest literature" (196). In 1969, Donald B. Gibson took Baldwin to task for what he perceived as his misreading of *Native Son;* Donald B. Gibson, "Wright's Invisible Native Son," collected in *The Critical Response to Richard Wright*, ed. Robert J. Butler (Westport, Conn.: Greenwood, 1995), 35–42.

4. Baldwin, *Notes of a Native Son*, 33, 27. In 1987, Bernard W. Bell revisited Baldwin's position when he asserted: "Wright intellectually rejects both the concept of Black consciousness and the values of Afro-American culture. . . . Wright's unqualified rejection of the viability of Black folk culture [religion, language, music, and humor] as a way of maintaining or changing arrangements of status, power, and identity in a hostile environment is intellectually, politically, and morally untenable for many." Bernard W. Bell, *The Afro-American Novel and Its Tradition* (Amherst: University of Massachusetts Press, 1987), 155, 165, 166.

5. Irving Howe, "Black Boys and Native Sons," *Dissent* 10 (Autumn 1963): 353–68; quotation at 354–55.

6. Ellison, *Shadow and Act*, 124, 120; emphasis in original. Interestingly, for most of the essay, Ellison wrote about himself in third person. That distancing strategy, designed perhaps to suggest objectivity, is nonetheless disconcerting at times.

7. The Wright scholar Keneth Kinnamon provides research on criticism devoted to Wright and *Native Son* in *A Richard Wright Bibliography: Fifty Years of Criticism and Commentary, 1933–1982* (Westport, Conn.: Greenwood, 1988). In 1940, when *Native Son* was published, there were 1,005 mentions, reviews, essays, and critical commentaries on Wright's work. After Wright's expatriation to France, such publications did not exceed 400 for any year before the publication of Kinnamon's volume.

8. I emphasize "few" because, as the Black Arts Movement scholar Howard Rambsy II points out, some of the writers of the sixties were involved in reclaiming Wright's work, and some contributed to the special issue of *Negro Digest* that was devoted to Wright. Though Rambsy notes that Wright was "a respected figure among the writers," there are still major divergences in their philosophies and works. See Howard Rambsy II, *The Black Arts Enterprise and the Production of African American Poetry* (Ann Arbor: University of Michigan Press, 2011), 5. Rambsy also notes that Amiri Baraka, one of the architects of the Black Aesthetic, did not voice new sentiments in what he believed writers of African descent should accomplish. Instead, Baraka "echoed sentiments expressed by preceding generations of Black writers, including Langston Hughes, Richard Wright, and Ralph Ellison. What distinguished Baraka, however, was the context in which he was writing"; Rambsy, *The Black Arts Enterprise*, 140.

9. Russell Carl Brignano, *Richard Wright: An Introduction to the Man and His Works* (Pittsburgh: University of Pittsburgh Press, 1970), 172; Margaret Walker, "Richard Wright," in *Richard Wright: Impressions and Perspectives*, ed. David Ray and Robert M. Farnsworth (Ann Arbor: University of Michigan Press, 1971), 65–66. For a detailed discussion of the complexities of the relationship between Wright and Walker, see Maryemma Graham, *The House Where My Soul Lives: The Life of Margaret Walker* (New York: Oxford University Press, 2022), especially chapter 11, titled "Dear Dick."

10. Nikki Giovanni, *Black Feeling Black Talk Black Judgement* (New York: William Morrow, 1970), 19–20; emphasis in original. Other poems in the volume carry similar tones of Blacks resisting the nonviolent approach to progress of Martin Luther King, Jr., and taking up arms for freedom. See especially the quietly controlled rage of "Reflections on April 4, 1968."

11. Sonia Sanchez, *We a BaddDDD People* (Detroit: Broadside, 1970), 59.

12. Rambsy, *The Black Arts Enterprise*, 5.

13. Sam Greenlee, *The Spook Who Sat by the Door* (New York: Richard Baron, 1969). Not only was Greenlee's novel popular with readers, but it was also made into a movie.

14. In a fascinating echo of *Native Son,* a couple of the young men "play white" in imitating an interaction between a white master and an enslaved Black person who does not want to be freed when Emancipation comes (114). Greenlee's young characters are keenly politically aware and are poking fun at the many plantation movies that were the rage in the sixties. Their purposeful imitation contrasts sharply with the vacuous imitation of Bigger and his friend Gus.

15. Larry Neal, "The Black Arts Movement," *Drama Review* 12, no. 4 (Summer 1968): 28–39. Hoyt W. Fuller, in "Contemporary Negro Fiction," *Southwest Review*

50, no. 4 (Autumn 1965): 321–35, contends that "in spirit," "the contemporary Negro novelist and playwright is the heir of Richard Wright, one of the century's most powerful literary craftsmen" (329).

CHAPTER 5. A Controversial Classic

1. Consider, for example, the literary scholar Florence Howe's sharing of her experiences teaching *Native Son*, in "Feminism, Fiction, and the Classroom," *Soundings: An Interdisciplinary Journal* 55, no. 4 (Winter 1972): 381–84.

2. Michele Wallace, in *Black Macho and the Myth of the Super Woman*, which was published originally in 1969, offers only brief mention when she asserts that "Richard Wright's *Native Son* was the starting point of the black writer's love affair with Black Macho" (New York: Verso, 1999), 55. Thus undeveloped, readers can only speculate about what kind of feminist analysis might have ensued from Wallace.

3. Sherley Anne Williams, "Papa Dick and Sister-Woman: Reflections on Women in the Fiction of Richard Wright," in *American Novelists Revisited: Essays in Feminist Criticism*, ed. Fritz Fleischmann (Boston: G. K. Hall, 1982), 395, 396. Williams concludes that Aun Sue in "Bright and Morning Star," one of the novellas in *Uncle Tom's Children* (1938), is perhaps the most fully drawn of Wright's Black female characters. About Wright's not being able to "imagine a constructive role" for his female characters, readers need but contemplate Sarah in his "Long Black Song" to meditate on the significance of this statement. Sarah is cast as undermining Silas's desire to move up in the world in his version of the American Dream. However, Sarah perhaps escapes from Wright's intent to denigrate her and achieves a qualified measure of agency. See Trudier Harris, "Peace in the War of Desire: Richard Wright's 'Long Black Song,'" *CLA Journal* 56, no. 3 (2013): 188–208.

4. Williams, "Papa Dick and Sister-Woman," 413, 396, 397.

5. Calvin Hernton, "The Sexual Mountain and Black Women Writers," *Black American Literature Forum* 18, no. 4 (Winter 1984): 139; Arnold Rampersad, "Introduction" to *Richard Wright: A Collection of Critical Essays* (Englewood Cliffs, N.J.: Prentice Hall, 1995), 1. Hernton credits only James Baldwin with sensitive portrayals of Black women.

6. In "Native Sons and Foreign Daughters," I argue that Bessie becomes mere evidence in the state's case against Bigger Thomas; *New Essays on Wright's Native Son*, ed. Keneth Kinnamon (Cambridge University Press, 1990), 63–84.

7. For a broad historical survey of domestic violence—from antebellum days through the late twentieth century—and the privacy and acquiescence that

surrounds it, see Reva G. Siegel, "'The Rule of Love': Wife Beating as Prerogative and Privacy," *Yale Law Journal* 105 (1995–1996): 2117–2207.

8. Sondra Guttman, "What Bigger Killed For: Rereading Violence Against Women in *Native Son*," *Texas Studies in Literature and Language* 43, no. 2 (Summer 2001): 182.

9. Wright, *Native Son*, 183–84.

10. Wright, *Native Son*, 233–34; emphasis in original. For a compelling and detailed discussion of Bigger's desire for Mary and his rape of Bessie and what those mean for "the myth of the black rapist" and the politics that Wright espouses in the novel, see Guttman, "What Bigger Killed For," 169–93.

11. Carol E. Henderson, "Notes from a Native Daughter: The Nature of Black Womanhood in *Native Son*," in *Richard Wright's Native Son*, ed. Ana Maria Fraile (Amsterdam: Rodopi, 2007), 55.

12. Henderson, "Notes from a Native Daughter," 61. For a representative sampling of essays across decades that treat female-centered issues in the novel, see Maria K. Mootry, "Bitches, Whores, and Woman Haters: Archetypes and Typologies in the Art of Richard Wright," in *Richard Wright: A Collection of Critical Essays*, ed. Richard Macksey and Frank E. Moorer (Englewood Cliffs, N.J.: Prentice Hall, 1984), 117–27; Alan W. France, "Misogyny and Appropriation in *Native Son*," *Modern Fiction Studies* 34, no. 3 (Autumn 1988): 413–23; Barbara Johnson, "The Re(a)d and the Black," in *Richard Wright: Critical Perspectives Past and Present*, ed. Henry Louis Gates, Jr., and K. A. Appiah (New York: Amistad, 1993), 149–55; Farah Jasmine Griffin, "On Women, Teaching, and *Native Son*," in *Approaches to Teaching Wright's Native Son*, ed. James A. Miller (New York: MLA, 1997), 75–80; and Shana A. Russell, "Wright and African American Women," in *Richard Wright in Context*, ed. Michael Nowlin (Cambridge University Press, 2021), 77–86.

13. Kimberly Drake, "The Meaning of Rape in Richard Wright's *Native Son*," in *Richard Wright: Critical Insights*, ed. Kimberly Drake (Amenia, N.Y.: Salem, 2019), 18–41; quotations at 32, 33.

14. Andrew Warnes, "Fatal Eyeballing: Sex, Violence, and Intimate Voyeurism in Richard Wright's *Native Son*," in *The Centrality of Crime Fiction in American Literary Culture*, ed. Alfred Bendixen (New York: Routledge, 2017), 161–81; quotation at 161–62. Interestingly, Warnes does not offer commentary on Bessie Mears, which shows yet again that Black women can never be the American ideal in film or in fiction. Notably, this erasure is less Warnes's fault than the tradition from which he has elected to make his commentary. Nonetheless, Bessie's erasure is as poignant here as it is when Bigger kills Bessie and essentially forgets about her until Buckley has her body brought into the courtroom. Warnes goes against the grain of conventional Wright criticism with this comment about

Mary's death: "On a literal, even legal, level, this murder is in no way inadvertent. The smothering is purposeful and meant to kill, and *Native Son* throughout remains at pains to emphasize the physical force that Bigger is bringing to the task" (167). Warnes does admit, however, that there might be "another level" at which the death is "in some way, unintentional."

15. Eldridge Cleaver, "Notes on a Native Son," in *Soul on Ice* (New York: Delta, 1992; originally published in 1968), 134; Maryemma Graham, "Introduction," *Callaloo* 9 (Summer 1986): 444; Gates, "Preface," in *Richard Wright*, ed., Gates and Appiah, xi; Rampersad, ed., *Richard Wright: A Collection*, 1.

16. See, for example, Patricia Tuitt, "Law and Violence in Richard Wright's *Native Son*," in *Law and Critique* 11 (2000): 201–17; Keneth Kinnamon, *Richard Wright: An Annotated Bibliography of Criticism and Commentary, 1983–2003* (Jefferson, N.C.: McFarland, 2006).

17. Keneth Kinnamon, "A Selective Bibliography of Wright Scholarship and Criticism, 1983–1988," *Mississippi Quarterly* 42, no. 4 (Fall 1989): 451–78; Harold Bloom, ed., *Bigger Thomas* (New York: Chelsea House, 1990); *Obsidian* 11, no. 2, Special Issue: Richard Wright (Fall/Winter 2010). The *CLA Journal* had produced such a special issue as early as 1969. I still have my T-shirt from the University of Mississippi conference. Wright's oldest daughter, Julia, has consistently attended programs in the United States designed to honor her father, especially those that Maryemma Graham organized at the University of Kansas.

18. Drake, "The Meaning of Rape," 19.

19. Briana Whiteside, "Multiple Strands of Resistance: Teaching African American Literature in a Maximum-Security Prison," in *Teaching with Tension: Race, Resistance, and Reality in the Classroom,* ed. Philathia Bolton, Cassander L. Smith, and Lee Bebout (Evanston, Ill.: Northwestern University Press, 2019), 87–101. I was invited to make the presentation on *Native Son* at the SAMLA convention in Atlanta, which I happily did.

CHAPTER 6. Bigger on Bigger

1. Wright, *Native Son*, 16, 17; emphasis in original; King James Bible, Job 23:2. For a brief discussion of the epigraph, see Jerold J. Savory, "Bigger Thomas and the Book of Job," *Negro American Literature Forum*, 9, no. 2 (Summer 1975): 55–56.

2. Kinnamon comments on the ironic use of Christian imagery in the text, including considering Bigger as a Christ figure; Kinnamon, *Emergence of Richard Wright*, 136–38.

3. A flying motif recurs in African American literature, from the mythical Flying Africans that people the works of Toni Morrison (*Song of Solomon*) and Paule Marshall (*Praisesong for the Widow*) to the literal references to planes and

flight in Ralph Ellison's short story "Flying Home," and Amiri Baraka's poem "Black Art." Even Malcolm X referenced the significance of planes when he discussed in a 1963 speech his refusal to be drafted because if he had a plane full of bombs, he would probably find the enemy a lot closer than Vietnam.

4. Wright, *Native Son*, 17.

5. Wright, *Native Son*, 20; ellipses in original.

6. Wright, *Native Son*, 71; ellipses in original.

7. Wright, *Native Son*, 116, 117.

8. Wright, *Native Son*, 145.

9. Wright, *Native Son*, 152.

10. Wright, *Native Son*, 172.

11. Wright, *Native Son*, 227; ellipses in original.

12. Wright, *Native Son*, 179.

13. Joseph T. Skerrett, Jr., notes: "Bessie is an oasis of motherly comfort in Bigger's world," which might be superficially applicable, but does a man have sex with his mother? Skerrett, "Composing Bigger: Wright and the Making of *Native Son*," in *Richard Wright: A Collection of Critical Essays*, ed. Arnold Rampersad (Englewood Cliffs, N.J.: Prentice Hall, 1995), 34.

14. Wright, *Native Son*, 279, 341.

15. Wright, *Native Son*, 338.

16. See Donald B. Gibson, "Wright's Invisible Native Son," in *The Critical Response to Richard Wright*, ed. Robert J. Butler (Westport, Conn.: Greenwood, 1995), 35–42. Gibson argues: "The point is that Bigger, through introspection, finally arrives at a definition of self which is his own and different from that assigned to him by everyone else in the novel" (36). He asserts that "in the final pages the focus shifts away entirely from the social emphasis" as well as away from the murder-as-creation theme and into "whether Bigger will save himself in the only possible way, by coming to terms with himself. This we see him doing as we observe him during long, solitary hours of minute introspection and self-analysis" (37).

17. For a recent discussion of how naturalism and existentialism inform *Native Son*, viewed through the image of blindness that pervades the text, see Ian Afflerbach, "Liberalism's Blind Judgment: Richard Wright's *Native Son* and the Politics of Reception," *Modern Fiction Studies* 61, no. 1 (Spring 2015): 90–113.

18. Wright, *Native Son*, 349, 350; emphasis and second ellipsis in original.

19. Wright, *Black Boy*, 263.

20. Wright, *Native Son*, 353.

21. James Baldwin, "Sonny's Blues," in *Going to Meet the Man* (New York: Vintage, 1995), 104.

22. As Robert Butler observes, Max errs in referring to Bigger as a "boy," for

that labeling earns Bigger "no special legal status. Quite the contrary, the word *boy* worsens matters for him, evoking the age-old stereotype of the irresponsible, unpredictably violent Black male who can *never* grow up and therefore can never be rehabilitated in prison." Butler, "The Loeb and Leopold Case: A Neglected Source for Richard Wright's *Native Son*," *African American Review* 39, no. 4 (Winter 2005): 565; emphasis in original.

23. Wright, *Native Son,* 358.

24. Wright, *Native Son,* 429; emphasis in original.

25. Jerry H. Bryant also notes what Bigger has learned: "But his own violence, his trial, and the final failure of Max to guess at what Bigger needs demonstrates the nature of the human condition—a lonely passage through a meaningless world in which the only salvation lies in the discovery and acceptance of one's self. . . . But if there is illumination in this for Wright, there is also the horror that Bigger had to kill to learn this, the horror in discovering how far humans will go, when pushed, to save themselves." Bryant, "The Violence of *Native Son,*" in *Richard Wright: A Collection of Critical Essays,* ed. Arnold Rampersad (Englewood Cliffs, N.J.: Prentice Hall, 1995), 22.

26. Ralph Ellison, *Invisible Man* (New York: Vintage, 1995), 266, 66; emphasis in original.

27. An exception to this often-cited Wrightian dismissal of African American folk culture is that Wright truly appreciated the blues. He wrote several blues songs and even assisted in getting some recorded. Compare Bigger's blues to what Edward A. Watson argues in "Bessie's Blues," in *Richard Wright: Impressions and Perspectives,* ed. David Ray and Robert M. Farnsworth (Ann Arbor: University of Michigan Press, 1971), 167–73. See also Kinnamon, *Emergence of Richard Wright,* 60–61.

CHAPTER 7. The Value of a Literary Life

1. Jerry W. Ward, Jr., and Robert J. Butler, eds., *The Richard Wright Encyclopedia* (Westport, Conn.: Greenwood, 2008), 272.

2. For a general discussion of the difficulty of transforming novels to film, with a special focus on *Native Son,* see Page Laws, "Not Everybody's Protest Film Either: *Native Son* Among Controversial Film Adaptations," *The Black Scholar* 39, no. 1–2 (Spring–Summer 2009): 27–33. For another discussion of the difficulty of such matters in connection with Richard Wright, see Jerry W. Ward, Jr., "*Native Son:* Six Versions Seeking Interpretation," in *Approaches to Teaching Wright's Native Son,* ed. James A. Miller (New York: MLA, 1997), 16–21.

3. Thabiti Lewis, "Bigger Still Haunts the American Imagination and Black Reality: Art with Purpose," *CLA Journal* 58, no. 3–4 (March/June 2015): 193, 194,

197, 210, Special Issue: Hands Up. Don't Shoot! Critical and Creative Responses to Violence Toward Black Bodies in the 21st Century.

4. Michelle Alexander, *The New Jim Crow: Mass Incarceration in the Age of Colorblindness* (New York: New Press, 2012), 189, 9. For interesting commentaries on southern territory about the impact of drug-related incarceration and deaths, see Jesmyn Ward's autobiographical *Men We Reaped* (New York: Bloomsbury, 2013) and her novel *Where the Line Bleeds* (New York: Simon & Schuster, 2008).

5. Two Wright scholars have offered commentary on what readings of *Native Son* and Bigger Thomas look like in the era of #BlackLivesMatter: Barbara Foley and Jerry W. Ward, Jr., "Richard Wright in the Era of #BlackLivesMatter: Two Views," in *Richard Wright in Context,* ed. Michael Nowlin (New York: Cambridge University Press, 2021), 348–57. Ward offers an engaging note in the context of influence, call and response: "Re-reading Wright's travelogues from the 1950s is essential for considering how far Richard Wright was in advance of Black Lives Matter" (356).

INDEX

African American folk tradition,
25, 51, 124–25, 138, 160n4,
166n27
African American literature
characters, pre-RW, 26–27, 40–41
flying motif in, 164n3
function of, RW on, 51–52
institutionalized study, post-
1960s, 102–4
pre–*Native Son*, 40–42
Protest Tradition in, xi, 19, 25, 28
purpose of, 25, 52–53
violence in, 146–47
"Alas, Poor Richard" (Baldwin),
160n3
Alexander, Michelle, 143
American Hunger (Wright), 11
American Literature Association, 115
Angelou, Maya, 136
Another Country (Baldwin), 90
Anvil, 16
art, social function of, 64
Aswell, Edward, 45–47, 77
Aunt Addie (*Black Boy*), 12–13
*The Autobiography of an Ex-Colored
Man* (Johnson), 40–41

Baldwin, James, 3
Cleaver and, 113
RW and, 19, 87–92, 124, 159n19,
160n3
—works
"Alas, Poor Richard," 160n3
Another Country, 90
"Everybody's Protest Novel,"
88, 160n3
Go Tell It on the Mountain, 19
"Many Thousands Gone," 88
Nobody Knows My Name, 160n3
Notes of a Native Son, 160n4
"Sonny's Blues," 134
Baraka, Amiri (LeRoi Jones), 95, 161n8
Bell, Bernard W., 160n4
Belton Piedmont (*Imperium in
Imperio*), 38–39
Bernard Belgrave (*Imperium in
Imperio*), 38–39
Bessie Mears (*Native Son*), 5
described, 6, 112
feminist critical commentary on,
xii
in film, 142
value of, 104–7, 109–10, 163n14